IMAGES
of America

STRUTHERS

One of the biggest celebrations in Struthers's history was the 1946 homecoming parade. Here is the Struthers Athletic Club float honoring the men and women of the armed forces. (Courtesy of the Struthers Athletic Club.)

On the cover: At the soda fountain of Bittner's Drugs are Bud Bittner and Alice Cooper around 1937 or 1938. Bittner's opened in 1925 at 329 Elm Street. The soda fountain attracted many and operated between 1925 and 1949. (Courtesy of the Struthers Historical Society.)

IMAGES
of America

STRUTHERS

Patricia Ringos Beach
in association with
the Struthers Historical Society

ARCADIA
PUBLISHING

Copyright © 2008 by Patricia Ringos Beach in association with the Struthers Historical Society
ISBN 978-1-5316-3280-9

Published by Arcadia Publishing
Charleston SC, Chicago IL, Portsmouth NH, San Francisco CA

Library of Congress Catalog Card Number: 2008923916

For all general information contact Arcadia Publishing at:
Telephone 843-853-2070
Fax 843-853-0044
E-mail sales@arcadiapublishing.com
For customer service and orders:
Toll-Free 1-888-313-2665

Visit us on the Internet at www.arcadiapublishing.com

*This book is dedicated to my family
and to the past, present, and future residents of Struthers.*

CONTENTS

ACKNOWLEDGMENTS

It is deceptive to have only my name on the cover when so many people helped to write this book. First, to the Struthers Historical Society, thank you. The care that you take of the history of our town is equaled only by your generosity in sharing it. In particular, Marian Kutlesa, thank you for your encouragement and mentoring as I began this book. Laddie Fedor, thank you for your help in reviewing and assisting in the completion of the book.

I would like to acknowledge and thank the following people who were informative, supportive, and inspirational as I put words with pictures: Dan Becker and Matt Maxwell, Davidson-Becker Funeral Service; Martha Bishop, Youngstown Historical Center; Rich Blackwell, Struthers Historical Society; Anne Boano; Michael Buchenic III; Thomas Creed; Donna DeBlasio, Youngstown State University; William DeCicco and Denise Simon, CASTLO Community Improvement Corporation; Lori Ficorilli; Steve Gerak; John Gingery, Struthers Athletic Club; Sam Jackson; Thomas Krestal, Struthers High School; Rosie Hollen; Dorothy McLaughlin; Julie Peterson and Lily Martuccio, Mill Creek MetroParks; Harold Milligan, milkman, mayor, engineer, and historian extraordinaire; Marianne Walters, the Elmton. Recognition is also given to the Struthers Bicentennial Committee, whose outstanding hard work produced the treasure *Struthers, Ohio, Cradle of Steel* and many memories.

Thank you to Arcadia Publishing and senior acquisitions editor Melissa Basilone. It was a privilege and a pleasure working together on this brief history of Struthers.

Thank you to my family and friends who believed I could do this. My parents, Rose and Paul Ringos, deserve special recognition as the link that pulled the book together physically, emotionally, and socially. And to my husband, Dan, simply, without his love and support this book would not exist.

All photographs in this book are from the Struthers Historical Society's archives, unless otherwise noted.

INTRODUCTION

There are many ways to document the history of a town. Important dates and events can be summarized, a timeline can be made, memories can be written, and stories can be read. This small volume on the history of Struthers blends bits of all of these. It is a scrapbook with narrative to complement the photographs.

There are many highlights in the chronologic history of Struthers, beginning when John Struthers discovered Yellow Creek in 1798 and returned there to live with his family the following year. The Cradle of Steel was born with the building of the Hopewell Furnace around 1803 as the iron industry pushed west of Pittsburgh. John Struthers suffered financial ruin after the War of 1812, but Marbletown continued sleepily with a wharf and two businesses, barely affected by the Ohio Canal. Thomas Struthers, John's son, bought back the family homestead in 1865 to honor his father and was instrumental in bringing the railroads and industry to town, and eventually Marbletown became Struthers by popular vote. In 1866, the first post office was established with A. G. Parker serving as postmaster. Industry continued to flourish: 1869 the Anna Furnace was erected, 1880 Summers' Brothers constructed a sheet mill plant, 1899 the interurban electric line reached Struthers, and the Youngstown Iron, Sheet and Tube Company was established in 1900. In 1902, Struthers incorporated as a village with Thomas Roberts as the first elected mayor. Also early in the 20th century, Lake Hamilton was formed, and telephone lines reached Struthers. Other major events in the history of Struthers include the 1946 Veterans' Homecoming parade, the 1948 Cradle of Steel celebration, a major snow storm in 1950, and the 1965 moving of city hall to Elm Street. The 1970s saw Astro Shapes established, a bicentennial celebration, Black Monday 1977 heralding the collapse of the steel industry, and in 1978 the formation of CASTLO Community Improvement Corporation to develop new businesses in Campbell, Struthers, and Lowellville. The 2000 census counted 11,756 living in Struthers, 4,704 households and 3,255 families. But although factual, there is more to the Struthers's story than these dates or numbers.

Another historical look at a town may be to recall a walk down the street as it was when you grew up. Harry Mallery, at the age of 90 in 1971, recorded "Bridge Street 1899," which is preserved in the Struthers Historical Society archives. In his memoir, he recalled the one-room district school building on the north side of Struthers as he walked down the steep unpaved road. He remembers the railroad tracks, the bridge coming toward town, and the trolley line. The businesses he recalled are the Struthers Furnace on the west side of Bridge Street and the Summers-Thomas rolling mill on the east side. These were busy, noisy places. Continuing toward town, there were businesses whose names may be forgotten and even whose function no longer exists, including C. C. Fitch's Hardware, W. T. Conklin's Wagon Scales, Charles Kimmel's Grocery Store, Cunningham Furniture and Undertaking Store, Andrew Lindsay's Barber Shop, Dr. E. A. Brownlee's office and home, Creed and McNabb's Grocery Store, William Stevens' Livery Stable, Ed Biddle's Butcher Shop, and Charlie Pulucci's Cobbler Shop. On this walk, Mallery gives a glimpse of a street lined with hitching posts at each store, the stage that came from Poland twice a day, a couple of saloons, a bakery, a drugstore, and a blacksmith shop. But again, there is more to Struthers than the buildings.

A hint of music accompanies the stories in this scrapbook. A Struthers symphony might tell a tale with Americana tunes of Stephen Foster, like "Oh! Susanna" playing in chapter 1, "The Early Years." Bruce Springsteen's ballad "Youngstown" might narrate the story of the rise and fall of the steel industry in chapter 2, "Cradle of Steel." "America the Beautiful" resonates when looking at Yellow Creek Park and Lake Hamilton in chapter 3. Dolly Parton's "9 to 5" might come to mind with glimpses of the daily lives of those in Struthers in chapter 4. "Celebrations" is heard with the laughter and cheering of family, friends, teams, and others in chapter 5. And in chapter 6, hum the *Jeopardy* theme song, as knowledge of well-known and little-known trivia is learned. These are some of the songs of Struthers. But there is always more.

There are the people. *Struthers* is a tribute to the men and women who have lived, loved, and worked there, yesterday, today, and tomorrow. The people within these pages are representative. In some cases, these are the only images that remain from a time past and preserved in the Struthers Historical Society archives. The images are the ambassadors to visit times and places we cannot. The book is not exhaustive, and I apologize in advance for any errors. My only regret is that there are photographs and stories that, because of the constraints of time and space, could not be in this book.

A town's history is more than any one thing and perhaps any text falls short. It is my hope that this book will continue to preserve the history of Struthers. Royalties from the sale of this book will go to the Struthers Historical Society to help in its mission of safeguarding the past for the future. All who read this are invited to visit. Finally, and above all, enjoy this book and be proud of home.

One

THE EARLY YEARS

The city of Struthers is located in the Mahoning Valley of northeastern Ohio. Although its story can start in a number of places, this one will start with Stephen Foster (1826–1864), the composer of such beloved songs as "Oh! Susanna," "Camptown Races," "My Old Kentucky Home," and many others. Foster was the nephew of John Struthers. Struthers married Foster's father's sister, and although she died before Foster was born, the family stayed in touch. During his youth between 1837 and 1842, Foster visited Uncle John Struthers on his farm both for fun and for economic necessity when the family fell on hard times. It is clear that Foster loved being there, and the affection was mutual. Struthers liked the young boy and predicted he would become "a very great man." This 1896 picture shows the Struthers depot with horses and buggies waiting for passengers or cargo on the left.

Celebrating the independence of the United States happens in towns all across the country. Here in Struthers, a 1901 Fourth of July parade winds its way through the streets, with people lining the dirt road waiting for the flags, banners, and wagons to pass. A few years later, marchers go past the old St. Nicholas Church on Lowellville Road (left). Ironically, Stephen Foster, the "Father of American Music" was born on July 4, 1826, the 50th anniversary of the signing of the Declaration of Independence. Later that day, founding fathers Thomas Jefferson and John Adams both died.

JOHN STRUTHERS
1759 — 1845

MARY FOSTER
HIS WIFE
1767 — 1819

From the country's birthday to the town's beginnings, Capt. John Struthers (1759–1845) of Pennsylvania stumbled through this valley while chasing Native Americans. In 1798, he purchased 400 acres in what was then Poland Township. The next year, he moved there with his wife, Mary Foster (1767–1819), four children, and an unmarried sister, building his first cabin just above Yellow Creek. He started the first flour mill in the township, which was also one of the first in the Western Reserve, and invested in the emerging iron business. In 1800 or 1801, his son Ebenezer was born, believed to be the first white male born in Poland Township. Although the War of 1812's battles never reached northeast Ohio, Struthers suffered heavy personal casualties: without manpower his mills shut down, his son Lt. Alexander Struthers (1788–1813) died in battle in Detroit, he lost all of his property, and he moved across the river. A survivor, in later years, he was elected sheriff of Trumbull County. His obituary declared that he was "one of nature's noblemen." This memorial monument for the Struthers family is in Poland Cemetery.

Tragedy struck John Struthers's children again in 1827. Daughters Drusilla (1805–1827) and Emma (1807–1827) drowned while crossing the Mahoning River in a skiff thought to have a defective rowlock. No one witnessed the fatal accident, but the girls left a shawl and bonnet on the bank awaiting their return. They were going to the post office in Poland to retrieve a letter Drusilla was expecting from her boyfriend in Pennsylvania. Her body was retrieved the next day from the bushes about one and a half miles from the launch site. Six weeks later, Emma's was recovered at the head of an island near the Dixon farm in Lowellville. Much later, this bridge crossed the Mahoning River connecting the north side of Struthers to downtown, Nebo, and other neighborhoods. Its location may be very close to where the Struthers girls drowned. (Courtesy of Marian Kutlesa.)

Thomas (1803–1892), the Struthers' sixth child, grew up working on his father's farm in the summer and attending school in the winter. He moved back to Warren, Pennsylvania, attended Jefferson College, studied law, was admitted to the bar, and was elected to the Pennsylvania state legislature. In 1865, he purchased all the property his father lost and subsequently laid out the village. (Courtesy of Baristow Photography.)

In 1832, Thomas married Eunice Eddy. This family portrait was taken about 1854. They had three children: an unnamed daughter (June–November 1834); Thomas Eddy (1844–1871), who died of typhoid fever shortly after his wedding; and Anna Eliza (1848–1880), who died after contracting pneumonia during a shopping trip to Philadelphia. Anna's only child, Thomas Struthers Wetmore, was the only lineal descendent of Thomas Struthers and died childless. (Courtesy of the Warren County Historical Society.)

Thomas Struthers, successful and entrepreneurial, was instrumental in bringing a post office and two railroads for the coal mines to town. Before this, between 1840 and 1865, canalboats stopped along this stretch of the river as part of the 90-mile system that ran between New Castle and Akron. During those years, the village of 80 people was known as Marbletown and had a wharf and two businesses. Struthers also partnered with other businessmen to open a hotel and the Anna Furnace. These endeavors brought jobs and supported work for this community. The village name was changed to Struthers by popular vote. Above is an early picture of the Pennsylvania Railroad depot. Below are workers outside of the Summers' Brothers Sheet Mill in 1884. It was hard, dirty work. (Courtesy of the Jewell Company.)

14

This home and dairy farm along Poland Avenue between Helena Street and Overlook Boulevard was first owned by William Creed, whose sons both started businesses in Struthers. Randall Creed opened Creed's Dry Cleaners, and Frank Creed opened a butcher shop and grocery store. The dairy farm was later purchased by A. D. Milligan, whose son Harold delivered the milk. Milligan's dairy was the first to pasteurize milk in Mahoning County. The house still stands on the diamond at Overlook Boulevard and Poland Avenue.

In 1899, electric lines more closely connected Struthers to surrounding communities. The first telephone was installed in the A. M. Lyon Drug Store to serve all of Struthers, Lowellville, and Poland. Struthers was an unincorporated part of Poland Township before it became a village in 1902. Thomas Roberts became the first mayor. The controlled chaos pictured above is at the corner of State and Bridge Streets during the early days of the automobile.

15

These are familiar views of Bridge Street. Above, buggies are going toward the bridge and river from downtown about 1905. At left is a later view from Bridge Street, "the big hill," looking toward the bridge and downtown with Hurtuk's Food Market on the left.

A new bridge was opened in 2000. Traffic across this bridge is no longer disrupted by trains, whose tracks anchored both sides of the old bridge. Pictures of its construction and the bridges side by side are shown.

It seems that school pictures have always been painful to take, at least for those in the picture. Pictured here about 1905 are second to fourth grades from the one-room schoolhouse on North Bridge Street near Highland Avenue. Students are (first row) Willie Lidington, John Morell, Willie Boehm, Sam Morell, Jimmie Hoover, Carl Zempky, George Smyrk, Andy Tompko, and Willis Gough; (second row) Barbara Lockshaw, Jennie Robbins, Jean Vanauker, Anne Byers, Mary Dugas, Katherine Guidos, Leona George, Louisa Maurer, Gladys Rook, Louise Frank, Margaret Coots, and Mary Roemer; (third row) Anna Sokolic, John Sabolia, Mike Guidos, Vicia Hilkirk, Lizzie Lucas, Mary Mound, Alice Cook, Mike Dugas, Effie Hilkirk, Mike Lockshaw, Nellie Zempky, and teacher Anna Gluck; (in the doorway) Erny Barnet, Rolland Livingston, and Roy George. Student Mary Roemer recalled that the school room had double seats, desk tops turned down, and books placed in a rack underneath.

18

Perhaps as early as 1801, there was a school in the Western Reserve started in a log house where Struthers now stands. Here is Elm Street School, a one-room building and the first public school in Struthers. It was located at the site of the present city hall. Boys and girls sat on opposite sides of the room and were punished by being moved to the other side of the room. In 1906, the one-room building was replaced by a school with eight rooms. Students who did not withdraw after the eighth grade attended high school here until the new high school opened in 1921. Throughout its history, Elm Street School also served as a hospital during the 1917 flu epidemic, as a soup kitchen during the Depression, and as a community center in the 1950s and 1960s.

Other one-room school buildings were replaced in the early part of the 20th century. Here is the new North Side Highland Avenue School with eight rooms, opened in 1908. Other schools built during this era include the South Side Sexton Street School with 10 rooms, opened in 1914; Center Street School with 12 rooms, opened in 1917; and Fifth Street School, opened in 1929. Manor Avenue and Lyon Plat opened in the late 1950s.

In 1920, the village became a city. This 1954 picture was taken at the Struthers Athletic Club during an election campaign. From left to right are (first row) George Nye, council president Joseph Repasky, Gov. Frank John Lausche, Mayor Harold Milligan, Sen. Thomas Burke, Rep. George Tablack, and William Harvey; (second row) George Novak, city solicitor Theodore Macejko, Ohio Supreme Court judge James Bell, third ward councilman Paul Zurrow, councilman-at-large Walter Zaluski, and councilman-at-large Mike Petruska.

The old home of town and city government was in this building on Bridge Street. Community concerns addressed by the government in those early years included intoxicating liquor sales, impounding of juries, livery sales and boarding stables, laying out new streets, granting contracts, and public office responsibility. The city administration building at 2 Elm Street opened in this location in 1965. The following served as Struthers mayors: Thomas Roberts (1902–1905), John Stewart (1906–1907), A. B. Stough (1908–1917), Horace Wilson (1918–1923), Hans Johnson (1924–1927), T. A. Roberts (1928–1939), William Strain (1940–1945), Thomas Needham (1946–1951), Harold Milligan (1952–1963), Bruce Papalia (1964), Joseph Opsitnik (1964–1965), Stanley Davis (1966–1970), Thomas Creed (1970–1975), Anthony Centofanti (1975–1979), Daniel Hurite (1979–1983), Howard Heldman (1984–1991), Daniel Mamula (1992–2007), Terry Stocker (2008–). (Courtesy of the Struthers Bicentennial Committee.)

Here is an early picture of the iceman, Charles Waldele, making deliveries. Later refrigerators came. Indeed the post–World War II affluence was made possible in large part because of the convenience of home appliances. For example, in 1940, just half of the homes in America had refrigerators, but by 1980, they were almost universal.

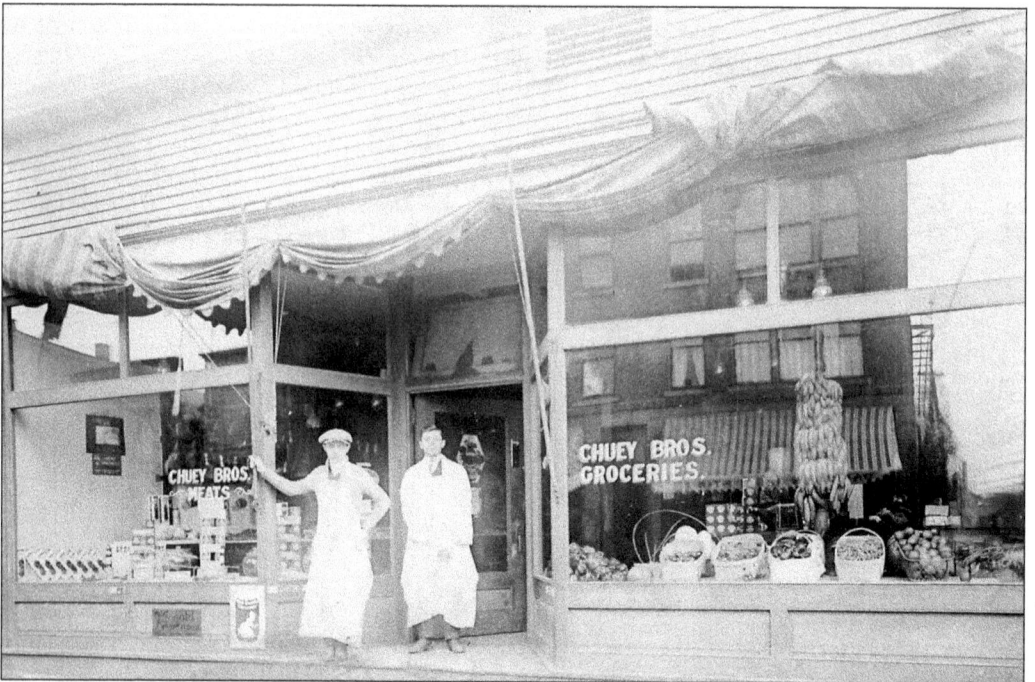

The Chuey brothers first opened a grocery store on the north side of town in 1909. The family business expanded with a general merchandise store opening on the south side in 1912. Here the brothers stand in front of the second establishment.

Vincent Feeney, pictured at left around 1919, owned the Polar Ice Cream Kitchen between the A-muse-U Theater and Penner's Furniture Store. The first Struthers bowling alley was at the back of this building.

Another downtown establishment from this era was a saloon owned by Charles Slaven. Later Paris Men's Shop was located in the building.

Alfred G. S. Parker (1852–1917), a former minister, opened the first drugstore in the village of Struthers in 1873 at the corner of State and Bridge Streets. He cleared the land, built the store, operated it for 23 years, and lived above it with his wife, Laura Cowden. The store also sold books and served as a post office. For his role as postmaster, he was paid an annual salary of $10.

A large tract of land on the north side of the river was first farmed by Kearn Milligan. Later known as the Snyder farm, John and Matilda Gilbert Frank rented the 93-acre farm from Matilda's uncle and purchased it after his death in 1900. John laid out the property and parceled it with improvements for selling. Here is a 1915 picture of Snyder Street on the north side.

While some Struthers neighborhoods like Gooseneck Alley, Pink Tea Hill, Gumboot Hill, Coke Alley, Dogtown, and Homecrest are forgotten, Nebo retains its identity decade after decade. It is a reference to Mount Nebo of the Old Testament from which Moses saw the promised land. Camp Nebo was on Center Street beyond Clingan Road and had a cabin near the hollow where Scout troops met. These Camp Fire Girls may have met there.

Here is a picture that dates between 1925 and 1930 of a Nebo gang ready for water activities, with fishing poles, oars, and bathing suits. Seen here are (first row) William Hanley; (seated on the ground) Charles (Chuck) Slaven; (seated) Fred Pichitino, Burt McIntire, and John White; (standing) Ed Slaven, Angelo Pichitino, and Louis Pichitino.

This home on Sexton Street was owned by the Creed family. Mabel Lyon Creed and her sons, Bill, Dick, and Tom, began the Maplecrest Nursing Home here. Built on the principles of dignity and worth of each individual, it is the only nursing home in Struthers. "When it was started, it was the only nursing home from Market Street to Pennsylvania," recalled Tom.

This picture shows Joseph Sokol riding his tricycle in front of Hurtuk's Food Market in the 1930s. Although the danger is difficult to discern from this view, this "big hill" was also commonly known as "suicide hill." It had a fierce bend, steep grade, and treacherous traveling in the winter. Many stories of perilous or near perilous misadventures are known throughout the area.

These pictures show the transformation of the Frankfort house that today is the home of the Struthers Historical Society. The original lot was bought from Thomas Struthers for $190. James John built the simple Gothic bungalow in 1884 for his daughter and her husband, Alexander Frankfort (1840–1930), Struthers's last surviving Civil War veteran. Their oldest daughter, Alma, was carried into the home when she was two weeks old and lived there for 93 years. She died in a nursing home at the age of 100. After her death, the house was donated to the historical society by her nephew Harold Mohr. (Courtesy of Marian Kutlesa.)

Renovations to recapture much of the home's original style took a three year, all-volunteer effort. As these volunteers will say, luckily only two layers of wallpaper had to be removed. The home's unique, diagonally placed central chimney allows for a heating stove in each of the eight rooms. (Courtesy of Marian Kutlesa.)

This 1939 Christmas picture captures a long-standing custom of the American Legion, the Christmas candy giveaway. Children stood in line to receive candy and a large apple. In the picture, notice Santa in the center front, the many children, and the old train station at the corner of State and Bridge Streets.

Two

CRADLE OF STEEL

Bruce Springsteen sang about the steel history of Struthers and the Mahoning Valley in his 1995 release "Youngstown," a history of heat, furnaces, and hard work. Steel is the malleable iron that can be tempered, treated, and shaped when obtained in its liquid state. The stories of the Hopewell Furnace, the Anna Furnace, and the Youngstown Sheet and Tube Company illustrate steel's impact on Struthers, "the cradle of steel." They do not tell the whole story, and that is left for other books to supplement. As Springsteen crooned, "Here in north east Ohio / Back in eighteen-o-three / James and Danny Heaton / Found the ore that was linin' Yellow Creek / They built a blast furnace / Here along the shore / And they made the cannon balls / That helped the Union win the war."

The Hopewell Furnace is given a lot of credit. Although the date is disputed, it was built around 1803 by Daniel and James Heaton on the west side of Yellow Creek about one and a quarter miles from the Mahoning River. This first furnace west of the Allegheny Mountains was envisioned by the brothers when they recognized all the ingredients needed to make iron, including iron ore, the red stones, along Yellow Creek; rich limestone deposits nearby; a large amount of timber needed for charcoal to melt the iron and stone; and the stream of water that would provide the blast, producing a hot fire in the furnace. The Hopewell Furnace is credited as the birthplace of the iron and steel industry in the Mahoning Valley and Ohio. Pictures show early steel workers and the Hopewell Furnace.

The beginning of the iron industry in Ohio almost coincides with the 1802 admission of the state into the Union. In 1807, Eaton (he legally changed his name from Heaton because of "superfluous letters") sold the pioneer Hopewell Furnace along with 102 acres of property and ore rights to John Struthers, Robert Montgomery, and David Clendenin for $5,600. In 1806, these partners also constructed the Montgomery Furnace about three-quarters of a mile from the mouth of the Mahoning River. The Hopewell and the Montgomery each produced about two and a half to three tons of metal a day. This metal was poured into molds for kettles, bake ovens, flat irons, stoves, and other articles. In addition to increased difficulty securing timber and furnace repair problems, both furnaces were critically impacted by the War of 1812, during which their labor force was decimated by the call to arms.

This is a picture of the Hopewell Furnace from about 1900 or 1901, with, from left to right, Burt Hickock, Wade Wells, and John Stewart. Begun in 1974, the Struthers Total Environmental Education Program (STEEP), financed by the Ohio State Department of Education with project directors Dominic Russo and Daniel Mamula, prepared a curriculum for outdoor education of nature and urban studies. In conjunction with STEEP, Youngstown State University Department of Sociology-Anthropology assistant professor Dr. John R. White directed an archaeological dig at the Hopewell Furnace site and, with about 25 students, uncovered much of what laid buried. As Mamula summarized the students increased awareness, "Earth does not need man to continue to exist but man needs earth to draw the simplest breath."

Carol Zanni marks a piece of ore found at the site during the dig. These furnaces used the heat of the blast to separate impurities from the iron ore, release the iron from oxygen, add carbon for strength, and reduce iron ore to its molten state. This liquid metal was poured into molds or "pigs" to cool and then used for various metal implements. The needed wood was cut from the surrounding forest and charred. The Hopewell Furnace, at peak operating volume, required nearly an acre of timber for charring each day. A design flaw, one side of the furnace was built into the hillside without use of a stone outer lining, allowed it to cool too rapidly and promoted inefficiency. Here are students on the STEEP archeological dig.

OHIO

HISTORICAL
MARKER

HOPEWELL FURNACE

The Hopewell Furnace, constructed by Daniel
and James Eaton in 1802, began operation in
1803. This blast furnace, the first in Ohio and
one of the first west of the Allegheny Mountains,
marked the beginning of the iron and steel
industry in the Mahoning Valley. The Eaton
brothers operated the furnace until 1808,
producing approximately two tons of iron per
day. Archaeological and metallurgical inves-
tigations suggest the furnace is the earliest
in North America known to have used a
combination of bituminous coal and charcoal
for fuel in iron making.

THE OHIO BICENTENNIAL COMMISSION
MILL CREEK METROPARKS
THE OHIO HISTORICAL SOCIETY
2003

9-50

The Hopewell Furnace site was honored by the Ohio Historical Society as a significant site of early Ohio industry about 200 years after it was built. A commemoration ceremony and historic marker dedication was attended by many on June 1, 2003. Mayor Daniel Mamula addressed the crowd. The Hopewell Memorial, donated by the Youngstown Sheet and Tube Lykes Corporation, stands beside Lake Hamilton about a quarter mile from the original furnace site. The memorial, designed by architect Thomas McIntosh as a steel ingot mold and time capsule, was dedicated on July 5, 1976, during the bicentennial celebration.

The memorial is engraved with these words: "A memorial to all those who pioneered and developed the steel industry in the Mahoning Valley. It represents the farsightedness of industrialists, the technical skills of engineers, the 'know-how' of mill operators, and the workmanship of labor. Through their cooperative efforts, steel has provided the means for growth and prosperity in this 'steel valley' community for many of our nation's 200 years." Within the protection of the ingot lies the time capsule. It holds gifts from Struthers residents of 1976 to those of the future, messages to a time and place they will never see. It is a promise with an opening scheduled for 2076. From left to right bicentennial commission chairman Gerald Schonhut and Mayor Anthony Centofanti receive the official bicentennial community designation from Congressmen Charles Carney and Thomas Carney.

The preserving of gifts for the future in the time capsule of the Hopewell Memorial was only one part of festivities that stretched through the bicentennial year. Other festivities included a parade, a picnic, and a presidential ball. Pictured above at the picnic in period costumes are, from left to right, councilmen Jack Vicarel, Fritzy Vicarel, councilmen Joseph Vlosich, Dolores Vlosich, Dorothy Hurite, and councilmen Dan Hurite. The grand prize winner and high school division winner for the flag design contest was Gary Galletta. He is shown below with the winning design.

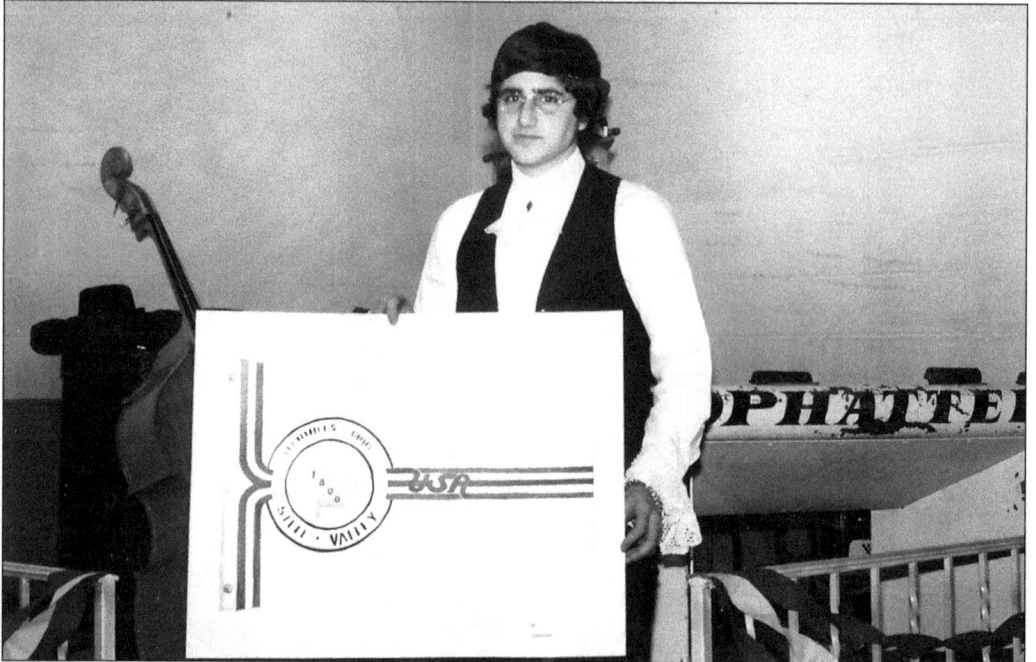

Another famous Struthers furnace was the next generation Anna Furnace, which stood close to the Mahoning River as a landmark for almost 100 years. This type of blast furnace used bituminous coal. This coal, also known as Brier Hill coal, split coal, or block coal, was mined in the area. The Anna Furnace was built in 1869 by the newly formed Struthers Furnace Company. This company was owned and operated by partners Thomas Struthers, John Stambaugh, Thomas Kennedy, and John Stewart; later partners were Daniel Stambaugh and H. T. Stewart. Anna was the first furnace in Ohio built specifically to use this coal. Named in honor of Thomas Struthers's daughter, it was the most modern of its time. This picture was taken in 1914.

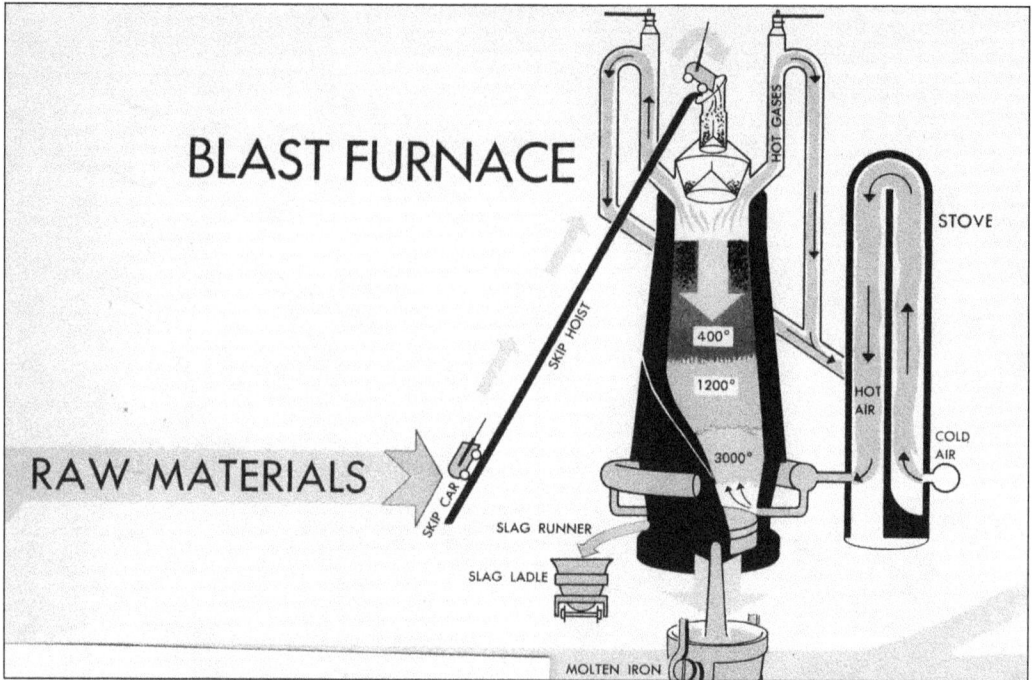

BLAST FURNACE

RAW MATERIALS

The blast process is illustrated here by a diagram from U.S. Steel. Near the bottom, pipes called tuyeres admit the forced draft or air blast. The process still dumped iron ore, coke, and limestone by huge buckets into the top stack to produce the molten iron that flowed from the tap. The closing-down operation was known as "blowing out" a stack. Several stoves supply heated air.

Initially the Anna Furnace had a capacity of 65 tons of iron a day, which increased over the years through rebuilding to 500 tons. Still in the 1960s it was one of the smallest and oldest in the valley. Anna last functioned in 1953 and was demolished in 1966. Product from this furnace supplied troops during the Spanish-American War, Mexican War, World War I, and World War II.

The Struthers Iron Company (formerly the Struthers Furnace Company) resurrected the iron industry in Struthers and spurred further industrial growth with the construction of the Summers' Brothers Company sheet mill plant in 1880 and the J. A. and D. P. Cooper Gear Company in 1888. Coal was mined in Nebo and around Fifth Street, near where Manor Avenue School and the Fifth Street Plaza would later stand, for industrial use. This home, built in the 1830s by Elijah Stevenson and now owned by the Bonish family, may have been the site of that mine. (Courtesy of Marian Kutlesa.)

The Youngstown Iron, Sheet and Tube became a major industry in Struthers when it purchased the Morgan Spring Company in 1909. Here is engine No. 101, with engineer Cecil McHenry.

Industrial giant Youngstown Iron, Sheet and Tube Company, later called the Youngstown Sheet and Tube Company, was organized on November 21, 1900, with authorized capital of $600,000 and 55 investors. The company was a large employer of not only Struthers residents but residents of the Mahoning Valley and all of the steel industry. George D. Wick was elected the first president of the company but only served until May 1902, when he resigned because of poor health. It was not until May 1904 that James Campbell (1854–1933) was elected as his successor. Campbell led the company for 26 years. His influence cannot be underestimated, and in 1926, Struthers's neighbor to the north, the former East Youngstown, was renamed Campbell in his honor. The Campbell Works, part of the Youngstown Sheet and Tube Company, employed many Struthers men. Three of its blast furnaces were built between 1907 and 1910, and a fourth one was built in 1913. Campbell stands in the middle of the back row with a group of managers and supervisors. (Courtesy of the Ohio Historical Society.)

The Campbell Works is seen in the background from a view of the south entrance, or Stop 14. It is easy to see how these stacks and others like them throughout the Mahoning Valley contributed to significant air and water pollution. Efforts to clean the environment and keep the economic advantages of jobs the steel industry provided stimulated debates without easy answers.

Italians and Slovaks were dominant groups to settle in Struthers. To help with finances, many recall taking in boarders. Three boarders might even share the same bed while they worked different shifts. The women also took in washing and ironing. This housing, known as the Highview Plat on Wilson, Creed, and Fifth Streets, was owned and developed by the Youngstown Sheet and Tube Company through its Buckeye Land Company.

Times of prosperity alternated with times of economic hardship. From Robert Bruno's book *Steelworker Alley*, Tony Nocera gives this account: "In the old days, foremen would pick the guys they wanted from a lineup outside the plant gate. You would pack a lunch and go out for the eight to four shift. If you didn't get picked, you went back out at four with your lunch, which was now your dinner. If you still didn't get chosen, you came back out at midnight. Your lunch was now your breakfast. While day after day I didn't get picked. One day I didn't go out on night shift. The next morning the foreman asked me where I was the night before. I told him, 'You never pick me so I didn't come out.' He said, 'I needed lots of men, you should have been here.' What could you say, you had no power and you needed the job."

Immigrants came to Struthers, recruited by the Youngstown Sheet and Tube Company's European offices, because of work. Family life was important to these workers. The health and wellness of the husband and father was vital to the family's survival. One resident recalled vividly in the late 1990s as a great-aunt was teaching her how to make haluski, an ethnic cabbage and noodle dish, when it was time to serve, the great-aunt admonished that the women could not eat. This elderly woman insisted that the men be "fed first" and called them in from the living room where they were watching a football game on television. At right is the 1929 passport photograph of Cvita Kraljevic Banozic (1906–1975) and her two-year-old daughter Milica, who came to Struthers from Yugoslavia following her husband, Mattimer, or Michael.

Without substantial financial strike funds to help the workers and their families, strikes were still not uncommon. Sometimes the issues were pensions or insurance benefits and other times they were less clear. Accident and death benefits were first offered in 1910. Chemical explosions, extreme heat, and unshielded equipment threatened the lives of those who labored in the mills. Unrest developed into rioting that erupted in East Youngstown (later Campbell) in 1916 and many buildings were burned. It was felt that only the calling in of 2,100 infantry protected Struthers and restored order. Pictured here are some of those troops. A strike in 1919 was called for a six-day workweek and eight-hour workday. What some call the most bitter strike was in 1937. During this strike, pickets outside of the Struthers mill attempted to burn rail ties to prevent freight car food deliveries.

In 1950, the Youngstown Sheet and Tube Company operated plants throughout the Mahoning Valley and in 18 other states, with principal producing plants in the Youngstown and Chicago districts. The Youngstown district plants included those in Campbell, Youngstown, Struthers, Girard, and Hubbard. In the rod mill (above) from left to right are Rocco Ambrozia, John Radilovitch, Charlie Marlik, Bill Jacobson, Mike Muszynski, Ed Glavic, and Clyde Rains. The picture below shows the fire protection squad, winners of the trophy for the 1915 annual field meet.

MRS. YOLANDA MARR
"Queen"
OF
THE "CRADLE OF STEEL" CELEBRATION AND VETERAN'S
HOMECOMING

MISS AMELIA SARICH
"Miss Struthers"

MISS LOIS RHODES
"Miss Mahoning Valley"

The "Cradle of Steel" was a dramatic pageant spectacle in Struthers that took place August 16–21, 1948, with queen Yolanda Marr, Miss Struthers Amelia Sarich, and Miss Mahoning Valley Lois Rhodes presiding. The written program extends Mayor Thomas Needham's welcome, "I am proud to be the mayor of this city during the time of this 'Valley Celebration and Veterans' Homecoming' and I take great pleasure in welcoming visitors to Struthers, 'the biggest little city in Ohio.'" A parade was part of the festivities, and here is the Yallech Lumber float.

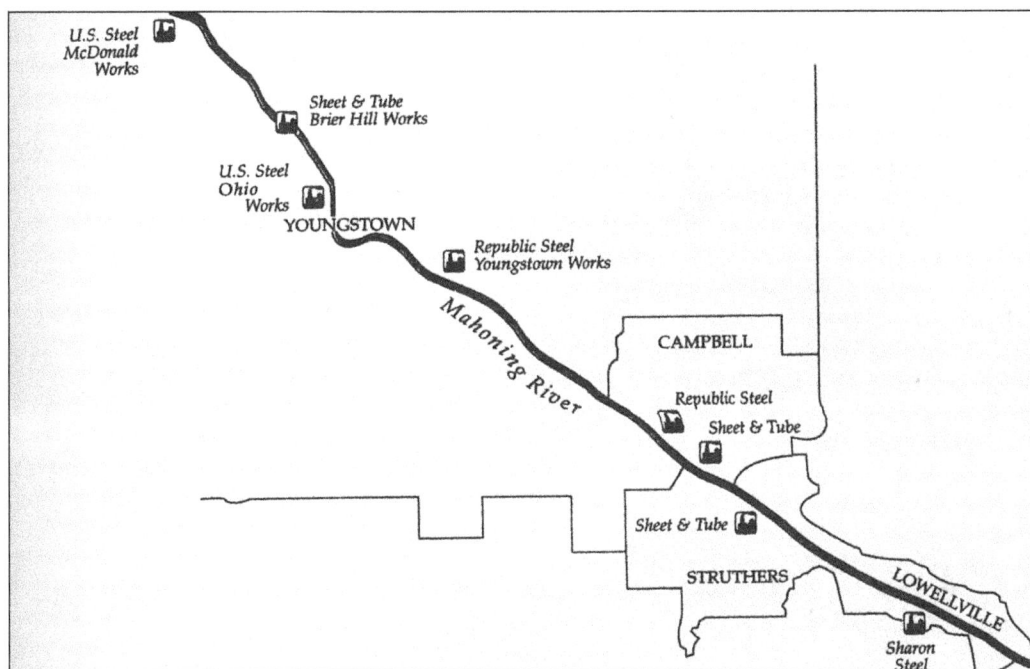

In 1976, approximately 970 Struthers residents worked for the Youngstown Sheet and Tube Company. This labor force received substantial paychecks, paid vacations from 1 to 13 weeks, medical coverage, life insurance, a retirement plan, and a survivor's benefit plan. Then Black Monday hit. On September 19, 1977, the Youngstown Sheet and Tube Company announced it was closing its mills in Youngstown. The official statement read, "Youngstown Sheet & Tube Co., a subsidiary of Lykes Corporation, announced today that it is implementing steps immediately to concentrate a major portion of its steel production at the Indiana Harbor Works near Chicago . . . The Company now employs 22,000 people. The production cut-back at the Campbell Works will require the lay-off or termination of approximately 5,000 employees in the Youngstown area." This map shows area steel mills. (Above, courtesy of Cornell University Press; below, courtesy of Hoop.)

An example of always being ready for the future, rebuilding, and opportunity, CASTLO Industrial Park is a nonprofit organization that was incorporated on March 21, 1978, in response to the 1977 closing of the former Youngstown Sheet and Tube Company's Campbell Works. Buildings that were not only abandoned but also vandalized have been renovated. Above is the Railroad Spike Mill built in 1915. Below is a picture of the entrance, taken about 1980, showing the old Struthers Works guardhouse on the left.

CASTLO's mission is to advance, encourage, and promote the industrial, economic, commercial, and civic development of Campbell, Struthers, Lowellville, Poland Township, and Coitsville Township. The CASTLO board owns and operates the 120-acre CASTLO Industrial Park in downtown Struthers and also is an active member of the Mahoning River Corridor of Opportunity, organized in 1995 to promote the redevelopment of former Republic Steel and Youngstown Sheet and Tube Company brown field property along both sides of the Mahoning River from the southeast edge of downtown Youngstown through Campbell to the Struthers-Lowellville border. Before and after photographs illustrate the Wire Mill, built in 1902, during extensive renovations about 1985 and below in 2007.

The economics and work that revolved around the steel industry were laced with social life. Friends, relationships, and memories were made. This 1926 photograph of Campbell Park, overlooking the Campbell Works with blast furnaces in the background, was the site of ball games, dances, swimming, and picnics. The park was owned by the Youngstown Sheet and Tube Company but located within Struthers boundaries. (Courtesy of the Ohio Historical Society.)

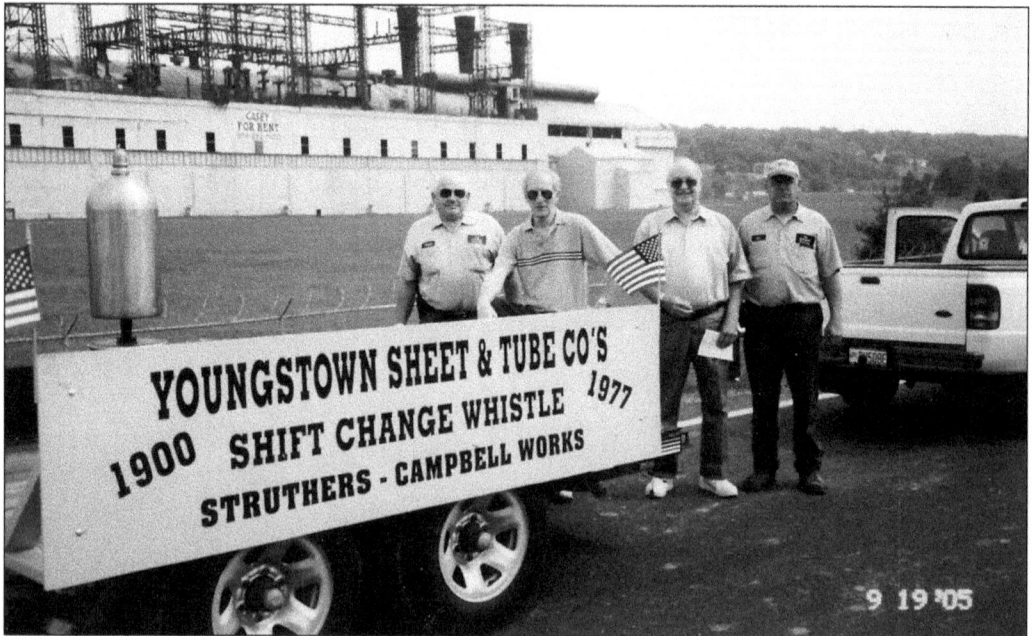

In the 21st century, the shift change whistle from the Youngstown Sheet and Tube Company is paraded with pride and nostalgia. Pictured from left to right are Charlie Schaffer, Rich Blackwell, Brad Ramsbottom, and Tim Daley. The whistle found a new home at the Struthers Historical Society.

50

Three

ALONG YELLOW CREEK

Although the spacious skies, amber waves of grain, purple mountain majesties, and fruited plains that inspired Katherine Lee Bates to write "America the Beautiful" were discovered during a trip to Pike's Peak, Colorado, rather than Struthers, the breathtaking beauty of Yellow Creek is no less stirring. It is easy to see how the natural bounty of Yellow Creek first captivated Capt. John Struthers, a Revolutionary War veteran from Washington County, Pennsylvania, as he chased a marauding band of Native Americans in 1798. He later purchased 400 acres, returning to the area to live with his wife and family. Struthers built the family log cabin on a knoll overlooking Yellow Creek, the site on Lowellville Road where St. Nicholas Church later stood. Even in the winter, the grandeur causes this hiker to pause and look heavenward.

Here a passerby stops on the bridge that spans across Yellow Creek from the downtown area. St. Nicholas Catholic Church sits high on the hill overlooking the valley. It was destroyed by fire in 1944. However, its steps going down to Lowellville Road still stand.

An early description of the city, written about 1910, boasts that "it has one of the finest parks in the country and the scenery is worth traveling miles to see." Yellow Creek Park is a 76-acre gorge area whose spectacular beauty is enjoyed throughout the year. Hiking, swinging, sliding, tennis, basketball, and picnicking are just some of the activities that draw young and old visitors. (Courtesy of Marian Kutlesa.)

Many improvements to the park were made later through the assistance of the Works Progress Administration program, including trails and retaining walls. The Works Progress Administration was the largest New Deal program/agency and was operated by presidential order between 1935 and 1943, providing jobs and income to millions of people across the nation during the Great Depression. (Courtesy of Mill Creek MetroParks.)

Improvements throughout the years and seasons have made even winter hiking a testimony to the park's enduring legacy. From its source, the creek flows due north into the Mahoning River, draining a water shed of about 46 square miles. Is walking along this creek so different today than it was when there was no city government, steel, or electricity? (Courtesy of Paul Ringos.)

The waters of Yellow Creek fueled the early iron industry. Frozen in the winter, they provided skating and hockey rinks. Arguably, one of the best-loved pastimes was swimming. Swimming in Yellow Creek is a pleasant memory that crosses generations. Older residents and earlier swimmers cooled off by jumping directly into the waters of Yellow Creek off Lowellville Road. The waters were clean, refreshing, and deep enough for diving. Although one can never know how many people swam directly in Yellow Creek through the years, even before there was a Struthers, eventually it became too shallow for swimming.

CTRUTHERS OHIO

These residents and later swimmers will fondly recall "the Birdbath" on Wetmore Drive, about halfway between the falls and Lake Hamilton. The Birdbath was a circular pool built in 1939 for $60,000. It had a diving tower with two high boards and two boards built on the island. A unique feature was its underwater observation room provided as an added safety feature. Swimming lessons were offered at the pool and many residents will remember some of those cool summer mornings with even chillier water temperatures, learning to put their heads underwater, float, crawl, and even dive, and that steep hill that had to be negotiated walking home on a hot afternoon. Pool concessions were often operated by high school classes as fund-raisers.

Swimming Pool in Yellow Creek Park
Struthers, Ohio

Today most visitors to the park will still agree with Joseph Butler's description in 1920, "The valley, or gorge, is of various widths, the hillsides steep and covered with evergreens, the fall of water in the creek abundant and resembling a rushing mountain stream rather than a Midwest waterway." The children having fun, from left to right, are Robert Boano, Marissa Buchenic, Kaylee Buchenic, Morgan Buchenic, and Rachel Drapcho.

In 2002 and 2003, the park served as a classroom for 3,000 students from Struthers, Girard, Youngstown, and Campbell. Coordinated by Youngstown State University, partners in the Mahoning River Education Project were the Mahoning River Consortium, Mill Creek MetroParks (which included Yellow Creek Park), local county soil and water conservation districts, Earth Force and General Motors Lordstown, Trumbull County Health Department, and local historical societies. (Courtesy of Mill Creek MetroParks.)

The management of this natural resource has not always been smooth. In 1974 and 1975, the Yellow Creek Park board was abolished by city council. Throughout many of the following years, the park was not maintained or improved. From 1981 to 1991, because of a lack of funds, the park was closed except for eight weeks each summer. On May 25, 1991, the park officially reopened under Mill Creek MetroParks.

Established in 1891, Mill Creek Park has approximately 2,600 acres, 20 miles of drives, 15 miles of foot trails, and a rare collection of gardens, streams, lakes, woodlands, meadows, and wildlife. Building on its environmental legacy and expertise managing urban park resources, the Mill Creek MetroParks preserves open spaces within the urbanized Mahoning Valley, including Yellow Creek Park. Seen here is Lanterman's Mill in Youngstown. (Courtesy of Mill Creek MetroParks.)

Financial resources were used to restore and enhance Yellow Creek's natural refuge. In 1991, $58,716 was needed to improve restrooms, the lodge, the pavilion, the playground, and the office. In 1992, $121,242 was used to construct a pedestrian bridge, install decking, dredge the pond, and upgrade the office. In 1993, $21,902 was spent to resurface tennis courts and expand park trails. And in 1995, $25,000 improved the lodge, the office entrance, the park trails, and the parking lot.

First recorded on county maps as a designated park in 1895, the city never had a deed for Yellow Creek Park. In 1940, city solicitor Theodore Macejko obtained the deed from Edward D. Wetmore of Warren, Pennsylvania, the sole trustee of the Thomas Struthers estate. Wetmore donated the land to the city in a trust to be used as a park, and this oversight of ownership was corrected.

58

Families often hiked to rocky outcroppings, carrying the tiniest ones, not only to enjoy the coolness on a hot summer day but also to take the family portrait. This portrait illustrates the changing clothing styles against the constant beauty of Yellow Creek.

One of the oldest homes in Struthers was at the entrance to Yellow Creek Park. Once known as the McKinney home, Shady Oaks, it was later owned by Joseph Sontich and even later served as the park office. It was demolished in 2008. (Courtesy of Mill Creek MetroParks.)

Each spring, the snow melts and the creek swells. Some years are worse than others. Watching and hearing this boisterous rush, one can imagine its power and the power of much larger moving water. In 1990, the flooding was high and the waters of the creek roared on their way to the Mahoning River, bringing along debris and sediment and spilling over the banks in many places.

Hiking along the creek one will cross Wetmore Drive and arrive at Lake Hamilton, seeing beauty and drama along the way. This map gives an idea of the route. It is a lovely three-mile walk from Yellow Creek Park to Lake Hamilton. (Courtesy of Mill Creek MetroParks.)

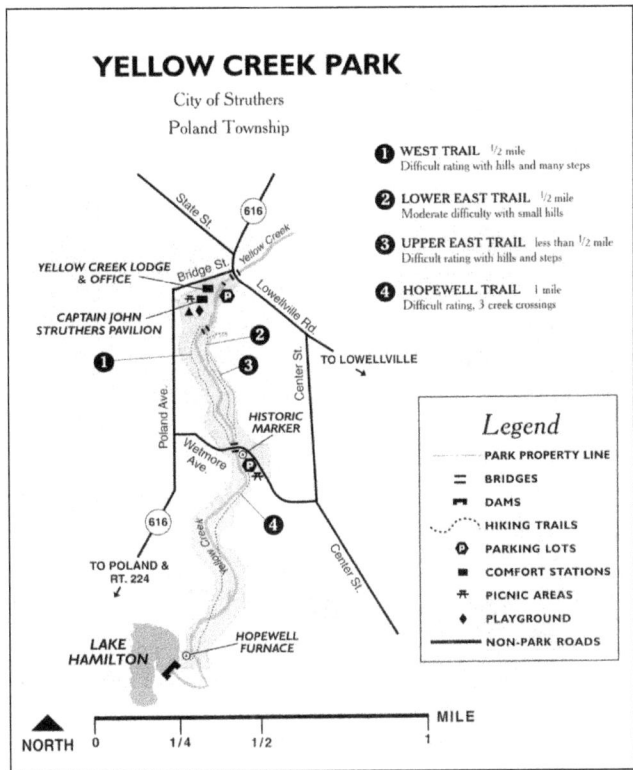

YELLOW CREEK PARK

City of Struthers
Poland Township

1. WEST TRAIL ½ mile
Difficult rating with hills and many steps

2. LOWER EAST TRAIL ½ mile
Moderate difficulty with small hills

3. UPPER EAST TRAIL less than ½ mile
Difficult rating with hills and steps

4. HOPEWELL TRAIL 1 mile
Difficult rating, 3 creek crossings

YELLOW CREEK LODGE & OFFICE

CAPTAIN JOHN STRUTHERS PAVILION

TO LOWELLVILLE

HISTORIC MARKER

TO POLAND & RT. 224

LAKE HAMILTON

HOPEWELL FURNACE

Legend

PARK PROPERTY LINE
BRIDGES
DAMS
HIKING TRAILS
PARKING LOTS
COMFORT STATIONS
PICNIC AREAS
PLAYGROUND
NON-PARK ROADS

NORTH   0   1/4   1/2   1   MILE

Not only do the seasons enter and exit with flair, as seen in these ice sculptures, but the rocks also fuel the imagination. It is truly a place for all seasons.

There are many landmarks along the trail. One is the Devil's Backbone. In this picture, the people are dwarfed beneath the Devil's Backbone. This ominous rocky formation is located about halfway between Wetmore Drive and Lake Hamilton. Along the way is the excavated Hopewell Furnace. The furnace is well known and is listed as a significant site of early Ohio industry by the Ohio Historical Society

The tranquility of Lake Hamilton is obvious to all. This tranquility hides its origins as a basin blasted to confine the waters of Yellow Creek in 1907. It covers about 101 acres and has a storage capacity of 800 million gallons. When water levels fall, one or two islands appear. In the early years, boating, fishing, and picnicking were popular activities.

John Ferguson (standing) was an early caretaker of the lake and dam. The masonry dam, built to form Lake Hamilton, was part of a three-lake project of the Mahoning Valley Water Company, later known as the Ohio Water Service Company.

The dam is of Ashler masonry and when built was one of the largest in the Midwest, the tallest and largest in Ohio, and pronounced by experts to be one of the finest examples of stone work in the United States. The dam has a height of 70 feet and a thickness through the base of 45 feet that tapers to a thickness of 10 feet at the top. It is 240 feet long, with a six-foot walkway across its crest.

Allen Charles Mastran was responsible for the successful nomination of Hamilton Dam, gatehouse, spillway, and aqueduct to the Ohio State Historical Advisory Board for designation on the National Register of Historic Places in 1983. Mastran did this as part of a Youngstown State University culture management class taught by Dr. John R. White, assistant professor of anthropology. (Courtesy of Ronald Garchar.)

When constructed, Lake Hamilton not only supplied water for residents and industry but also for fire hydrants. In 1908, a review declared that 20 Matthews fire hydrants be installed, giving the town adequate fire protection. Much credit for the development of this water plan for the Mahoning Valley Water Company is given to its leadership. In 1908, these principals were Lucius E. Cochran, Frederick B. Hamilton, Mason Evans, and James J. McNally.

Hiking through the park, the beauty may be more evident than the function. The aqueduct system was built to carry the pipeline from the lake to the town and its industries. This line is carried and runs as straight as possible, and all turns are made with long bends to reduce the friction of the water and avoid undue stresses. The course is tortuous, and it is necessary for the pipeline to cross the creek a number of times. (Courtesy of Ronald Garchar.)

The Canadian goose with its distinctive black head and neck and white "chinstrap" is a familiar, prolific year-round sight at the lake, migrating back and forth from the lake to surrounding fields daily. The birds are 30 to 43 inches long with a 50- to 71-inch wingspan and weigh 5 to 14 pounds. Although very aggressive in defending their territory, here geese gently greet young visitors to Lake Hamilton. In these 1990 photographs, Stacie and Kimberly Beach, visitors to Struthers and granddaughters of Rose and Paul "Kell" Ringos, feed them some old bread.

Struthers is a town of about five square miles with about 55 miles of streets. Many of its streets are named after villagers who originally bought the land. Some of these are Morrison Street, Creed Street, Wilson Street, and Perry Street. The first curbs were made from limestone mined in Nebo, near Perry and Katherine Streets. In this aerial photograph, the north side of the city is at the top and Yellow Creek Park greenery winds its way across the bottom. Neighborhoods, the park, and industry are all evident here in the early 1960s. (Courtesy of Gene's Studio.)

Four

NINE TO FIVE

In her song "9 to 5," Dolly Parton sang it loud and proud: "With folks like me on the job from nine to five." That is everyday life for most of the people who live or have lived in Struthers. And that everyday life makes for some of the most interesting moments. As Annie Dillard said a little differently, "How we spend our days is, of course, how we spend our lives." The Struthers Fire Department dates back to about 1908. First located in the Cunningham building on the corner of Bridge and Liberty Streets, in 1943, it moved to Elm Street, and in 1954, it opened the North Side station. Here firefighters John Prest and Robert Cherry pose in this 1930s photograph.

In the early days, the fire department had a two-wheeled wagon, Engine No. 20, purchased for $900 and pulled to a fire by hand. Around 1910, a horse-drawn wagon was used. A. D. Allen, chief from 1901 to 1910, is credited with training the first team of horses to work for the department. The Struthers Volunteer Fire Company is photographed here with a wagon and horses outside the Cunningham Furniture and Undertaking Company. The *Souvenir*, published about 1910 to raise funds for the company, identified the following members: Allen, W. M. Dehn, Mart Dittmar, Frank Creed, Louis Lawlor, John Ditmore, Fred Bird, Cyrus Cluse, Tom Roberts, Will Brown, Harry Miller, John Hake, Alex Stevens, Fred Barhoover, George Weathead, Clair Horne, Edwin Welsh, C. E. Kimmel, Alton Dickson, Enos Hum, and Charles Mundorf. (Courtesy of Rembandt Studio.)

The department's first fire truck was purchased in 1919. In this 1923–1924 photograph, above, it is seen with firefighters Hazen Becker, Carl Pantel, Clark Hoffman, Carl Vanauker, Russel Brown, Fred Dittmar, Charles Walldale, Charles Mohr, Mart Bird, Carl Menzer, Bob Cherry, Paul Velker, Bill Gosset, Sam Ludington, Karl Kurtz, Ottis Heldman, and Al Hull. Below, Ken Sabol takes the oath to become a fire engineer on April 10, 1995, from Mayor Daniel Mamula, as his parents, Pat and George Sabol, and Chief Harold Milligan Jr. look on.

St. Nicholas Catholic Church was established as part of the Cleveland Diocese in 1865. First located on Bridge Street, the earliest fire destroyed the tiny frame church in 1907. Later located on Lowellville Road, it is seen here before and during the second fire. In December 1944, an overheated furnace was blamed for completely destroying the second church building at a loss of $35,000. Then a 1967 fire at the church, now located at Fifth and Wilson Streets, resulted in damages totaling $150,000. This fire was started by a safecracker's cutting torch in the priest's sacristy during an attempted robbery. The fire destroyed the sacristy and altar with heavy smoke and water damage throughout, even melting the lead mountings of the organ pipes. More than 50 firemen from Struthers, Youngstown, and Boardman Township fought the fire.

Sylvia Lewis once said, "If you want your children to follow in your footsteps, be very careful where you put your feet." The churches in Struthers are an important footstep. The Christ Lutheran Church started in 1919 as a mission with two pastors serving out of Youngstown. In 1921, its status changed from mission to church. The beautiful brick church on Sexton Street was built with member contributions for $45,000 in 1929.

Founded in 1804 in Poland Center, the United Presbyterian Church is one of the oldest religious organizations in Struthers. It has been said that it originally had no artificial heat because members believed the pastor should provide all the fire. However, in 1820, a stove was installed. The founding Struthers families attended services there. In 1849, the log church was replaced, and in 1884, the new church was dismantled and moved to Struthers. A majestic stone building eventually replaced the older frame one.

In 1886, a Methodist Society was formed in Struthers, meeting for services along the banks of Yellow Creek in the summer months. The church at Sexton and Stewart Streets was known as the Struthers Methodist Episcopal Church. In 1940, its name changed to the Struthers Methodist Church and in 1968 to the United Methodist Church. These pictures show the church and its delegates in 1919.

From the humble beginnings in 1918 when six families met in the second floor of the village fire station, there have been three Baptist congregations in Struthers: the First Baptist Church at Morrison and Ohio Streets (pictured here), Struthers Baptist Tabernacle on Elm Street, and Pilgrim Baptist Church at McClure and John Streets.

Holy Trinity Catholic Church was founded in 1902 by 103 Slovak families under the spiritual leadership of Fr. Paul Herman. The first church, a small wooden structure, was built on Washington Street in 1907. The school was founded in 1910. In 1954, a new church was built of stone on North Bridge Street.

This picture shows the Struthers downtown business district. The Dollar Bank building is a landmark. In July 1902, the building was first opened as the Struthers Savings and Bank Company. It closed on April 3, 1920, due to mismanagement and misappropriation of funds. In June 1920, this branch of the Dollar Savings and Trust Company opened in the same location and remained open until 2003.

The Struthers Federal Credit Union has been serving the community since February 9, 1960. Begun as a credit union for school employees, it eventually opened to all who work, live, and worship within the Struthers School District. Seen during a 1988 ribbon-cutting ceremony, from left to right, are Helen Benton, Linda Krestel, James Trafficant, Rosemary Hollen, Rita Patrick, and Brad Ramsbottom.

Working is at least partly about the money and here is a picture of another financial institution that has stood on State Street since 1919, the Home Savings and Loan Company of Youngstown. Many older tellers at any Struthers financial institution remember the thousands of dollars that passed through their windows and fingers on "Sheet and Tube" payday. In the basement of the Home Savings and Loan Company was a barbershop. In this 1938 photograph are Clarence "Red" Hartzell (left) and D. W. Lee.

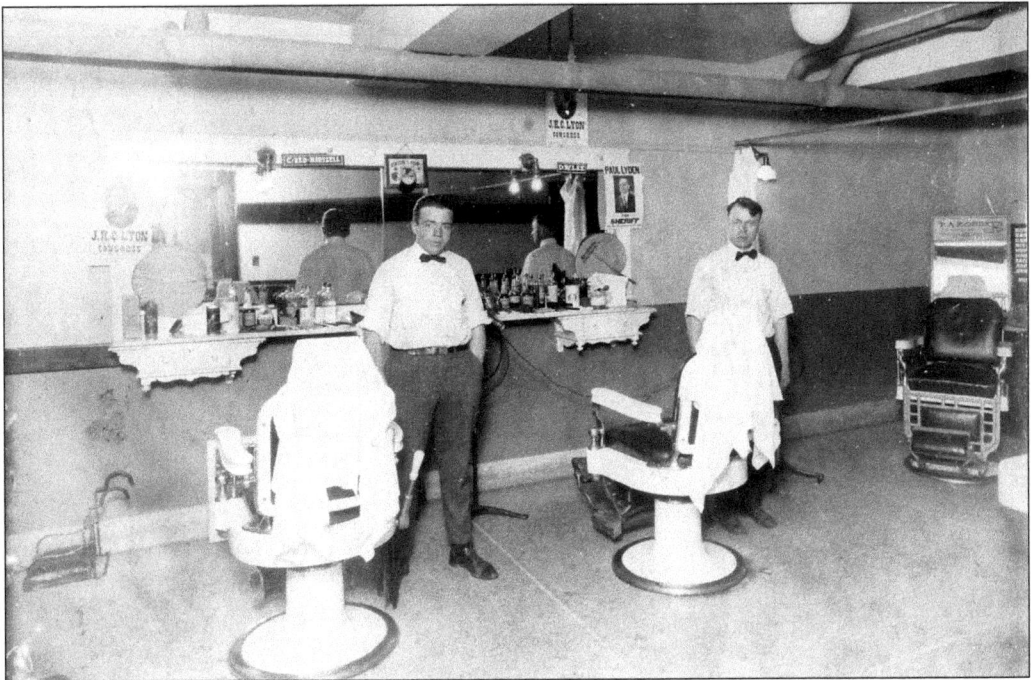

Here is a picture of the modern-day Hackley Pharmacy. It occupied the building on the corner of Poland Avenue and Sexton Street, which originally housed Wittenauer Pharmacy. The pharmacy or drugstore not only sold medications but Wittenauer's also had a candy counter that was a handy stop on any walk to the library.

Today the traditional shoemaker or cobbler has largely been replaced by the industrial manufacture of footwear. However, Ben Defendiefer Sr. started a shoemaking and repair business in Struthers about 1910. Here he and a helper stand in work clothes ready for the job.

In this picture taken about 1920, Cecil McHenry stands in front of his gasoline station at Bridge and Liberty Streets. It was the first gas station in Struthers. Although the price of gasoline is not seen, notice the sign for "free air" and the advertisement for Good Year Tires on the side of the building.

Here is a 1950s picture of Macejko Brothers on State Street. It was a family business founded in 1938 by brothers Steve, Dan, and Joe Macejko. The price of gasoline is not known, but it is a safe bet that it was not a self-serve station.

Davidson-Becker Funeral Home is the oldest in Struthers. Founded in Lowellville in 1896 by Dan Davidson and Jesse Cunningham, it operated from a storefront. In those days, embalming and visitation services were in the home of the deceased. In 1907, they opened a funeral home and livery firm on Bridge Street in Struthers. Later Cunningham assumed ownership of the Lowellville firm, and Davidson remained in Struthers, moving to the Poland Avenue location in 1913. After serving in the U.S. Army during World War I, Hazen Becker, Davidson's stepson, returned to the business. Between 1910 and 1915, it was the first in the area to use automobiles for the funeral procession.

In 1925, the first freestanding building in this area used exclusively as a funeral home was constructed. The building's many firsts included a dedicated embalming room, an electric generator, air-conditioning, and a drive-in garage. Hazen Becker's son Dan served in the U.S. Army as a paratrooper sergeant with the 82nd Airborne Division and upon his return in 1961 entered the funeral business. In 1962, the D. A. Davidson name was changed to Davidson-Becker. In 1999, Dan's daughter Kelly Becker-Rumberg became president and is the fourth generation to lead this independent funeral home entering its second century of operation. In this 1917 photograph (right) is Dan Davidson with Virginia McHenry. As a young boy, Dan Becker (below) stands in front of the firm's ambulance-hearse.

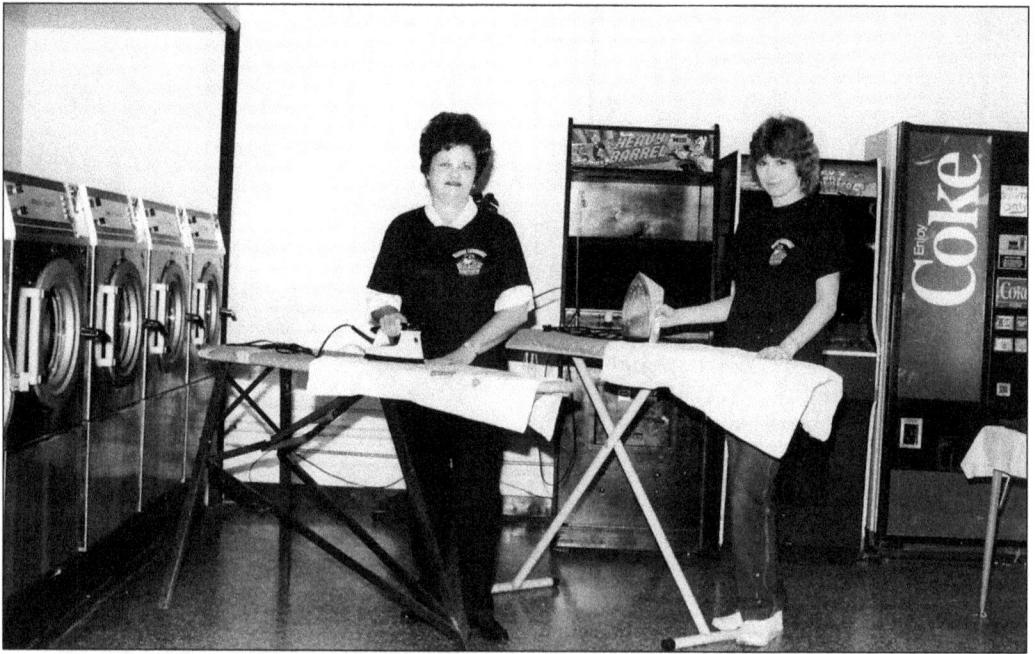

Not nearly as well documented or photographed is the work that women did. Above, women at the laundromat at Fifth Street and Midlothian Boulevard do the work. In a speech to Ohio women in 2003, Mrs. James Hopley described the situation: "For what have Ohio women been conspicuous? The answer is a simple one; Ohio women never were and are not now conspicuous. To be conspicuous has never been thought by them desirable. They have written; have sung; have molded in clay; have carved in stone; have had place and power; but forward, notorious, conspicuous in the common sense they have never been. In this their inheritance is revealed." Pictured below in a 1990 photograph is Sam Clemente in front of the Clemente Memorial Chapel and newly purchased ambulance. (Courtesy of Clemente.)

The business of food is important to any town. In Struthers, there have been family owned markets and larger chain stores. This is a 1991 picture of Stanton's market and staff. From left to right are Yolanda Polombi, John Toriello, ? Stanton, and three unidentified people.

This picture is of the 1986 ribbon-cutting ceremony at the grand opening of Frattaroli's Struthers Sparkle Market in the Fifth Street Plaza. The Frattaroli brothers purchased the store from Mahoning Sparkle Markets. From left to right are (first row) Mrs. Cesidio Frattaroli, Jerry Sullivan, owner Pat Frattaroli, Jan Frattaroli, Mayor Howard Heldman, owner Tony Frattaroli, George Stanko, and Tony Frattaroli Jr.; (second row) Bob Bivona, Margie Frattaroli, councilman Thomas Creed, Chuck Acri, and Robin Klughart.

Toriello and Sons grocery store was started by Emilio Toriello in 1918, and after his death in 1955, his children, Rose, John, and Raymond, assumed the responsibility of the family business. The store was known for offering its customers credit during the Depression and for being the first in Mahoning County to have a state liquor license in 1936. In this 1946 photograph, Emilio and Diamante Toriello stand in front of their downtown market wearing festival hats honoring the veterans' homecoming.

Second Class Petty Officer Michael Buchenic III, a Struthers High School class of 1977 graduate, is shown while in the navy (1977–1981). Buchenic was an aviation antisubmarine warfare operator stationed in Jacksonville, Florida. His highly classified service took him to Bermuda, Iceland, and Sicily, while tracking Russian submarines by air.

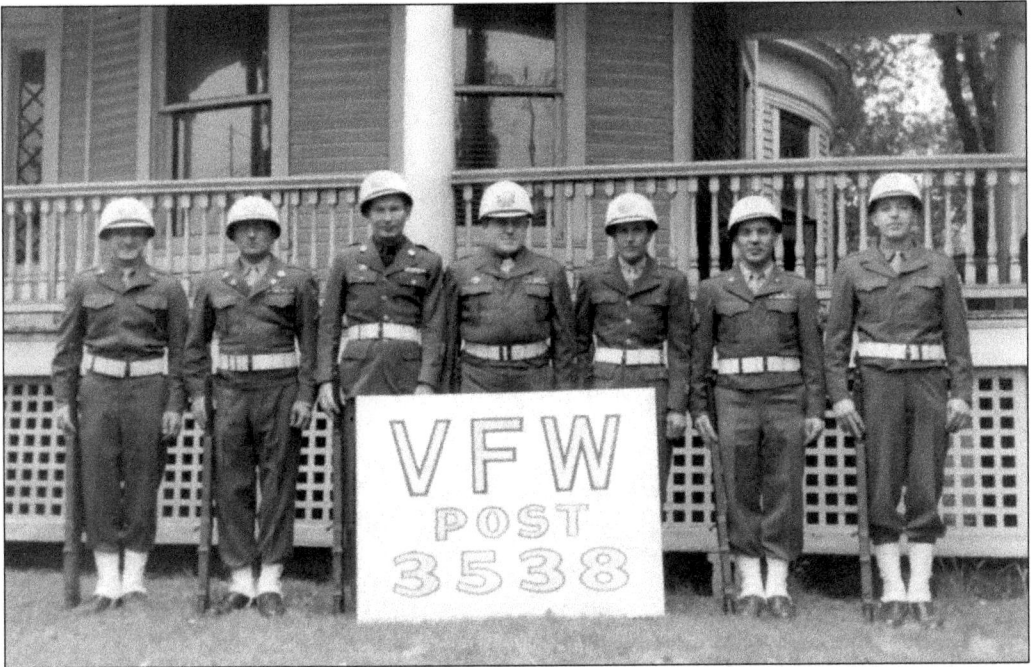

Throughout wars and maneuvers, people in Struthers and the local Veterans of Foreign Wars (VFW) support those who serve. Here is the VFW Post 3538 drill team posed in front of their first headquarters. During World War II, the Struthers Athletic Club published and mailed a newsletter. The *SAC News*'s inaugural issue was June/July 1943, and it was full of news about the euchre players, their military exploits, and where they were stationed. Young men from Struthers were serving from Texas to North Africa. Here on Memorial Day, an honor guard remembers those who have died with a gun salute and wreath tossing into the Mahoning River.

In 1979, Hopewell Cable Television came to Struthers and television was never again the same, as choices expanded from the three major network affiliates in the area, WYTV, WKBN, and WFMJ. The other change, of course, was the addition of a cable bill for resident subscribers. Here Don Walsh and Chuck Windsor work on the construction.

The original Struthers Sewage Treatment Plant was completed in 1961 under Mayor Harold Milligan. Located on Lowellville Road, the property was previously owned by Youngstown Sheet and Tube Company and Sharon Steel, which both deeded it to the city for $1 each. In 1985, construction was extensive, as the plant was upgraded and rebuilt. Seen here is Mike Sandusky. (Courtesy of Paul Ringos.)

Schools are a big part of everyday life and community. They are the students' workplace. Struthers High School was built at 111 Euclid Avenue in 1921 at a cost of $275,000. Twenty-one students graduated in 1922 as the new building's first graduating class. The auditorium seated 800 and was the site for many shows. It also served as a community center during World War II and as a church for the St. Nicholas congregation after it was destroyed by fire. In 1935, the basement was built under the school, with funding from the Public Works Administration program of Pres. Franklin D. Roosevelt's administration. Vocational classes and physics and chemistry laboratories were housed there. In 2003, that building was demolished and a new high school built. The track and football field can be seen at the back of the original high school. (Courtesy of Marian Kutlesa.)

In this 1924 photograph, young women are dressed in their gym uniforms, prepared to participate in an outdoor physical education class. It was not until 1925 that Struthers High School had a home football field. In 1930, the school had its first undefeated football team.

Located for years in the Fifth Street Plaza is Fiesta Hair Salon. Pictured from left to right in this photograph from 1989 or 1990 are (first row) Tina Perry and Joyce Palvov; (second row) Shirley ?, Dee Cavanaugh, Cybil Romeo, Ester Storle, and Tammy Sivarella.

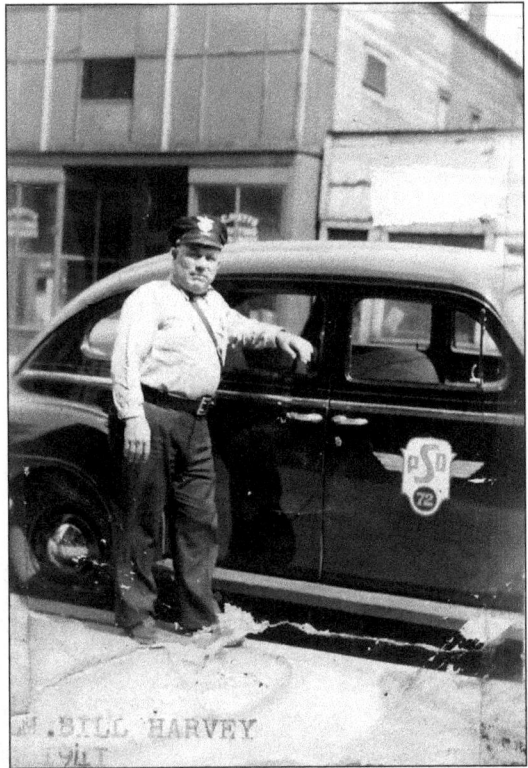

The mission of the Struthers Police Department is "to provide a safe and orderly environment for the community, in which citizens can conduct their business and their daily lives, through the best efforts of the department's personnel and the most efficient use of its resources." In the 1930s, Struthers had a population of 11,240 residents and very little crime. Chief Harry Davis credited his crew of seven policemen and the fact that the business district was between two railroads for the safe living conditions. Officer William Harvey stands next to a squad car in the 1941 photograph at right, as does Joe Gabriel below.

Dorothy McLaughlin, in this 1960 photograph, volunteered most of her adult life. She was the first Struthers auxiliary police officer and volunteered for the city in this capacity for 26 years. Always active in the Democratic Party, she received numerous awards and citations. (Courtesy of Dorothy McLaughlin.)

The Struthers Peace Officers Memorial stands at the edge of Lake Hamilton as testament to those who have died. Killed in the line of duty were officer John Harkins on January 5, 1952, and officer Raymond Darwich on November 16, 1952. Other officers who have died are also memorialized.

Five

CELEBRATION

Kool and the Gang sang it in 1980, "There's a party goin' on right here. A celebration to last throughout the years." People, families, towns, cities, and countries celebrate big and small events. This photograph is of the wedding party and guests at the January 31, 1928, wedding of Struthers residents Sophie Blasic and Joseph Ringos. Celebrating with the bride and groom are Mike Matuscak (seated, second from left), Betty Skvarka (flower girl to the left of the bride), John Ringos (seated to the right of the bride), Matt Zelinski (seated at the far right), Sophie Slannia Ringos (third row, second from the left), Mary Zelinski Spontak (third row, fourth from left), John Blasic (third row, third from right), and John Zelinski (fourth row, second from right). (Courtesy of Rees Studio.)

One of the customs at Struthers's weddings is the cookie table. Guests are served wedding cake and cookies at the reception. These have been baked by family and friends of the wedding couple. They are beautifully displayed and delicious. The varieties are endless and include traditional favorites like buckeyes, biscotti, thumb prints, cannoli, kiffels, clothes pin cookies, kolachi, pinwheels, cheregies, pizzelles, and butter balls. Every cookbook put together as a fund-raiser for any school, church, or club in Struthers will have these recipes. Holidays are also celebrated with food and fun. Below, the crowds are for the annual Easter egg hunt. The hunt has been held at Yellow Creek Park and, as in this picture, on the high school grounds.

The 1924–1925 Struthers High School girls' basketball team won the Ohio State tournament and went to the national tournament, reaching the finals only to lose 25–22. In 1925–1926, they were again state champions. That year, the Struthers Businessmen's Association underwrote the cost to host the national girls' tournament at the old Rayen-Wood Auditorium. They again reached the finals this time losing to the Pennsylvania state champions 22–20. That was the last tournament the girls participated in for a number of years because the Ohio State Athletic Association stopped interscholastic athletic girls' competitions. The 1924–1925 team, pictured from left to right includes (first row) Margaret Creed, Jane Anderson, Evelyn Conway, Bessie Albrecht, Vivian Troby, Matilda Hetrick, and Velma Smith; (second row) manager Blanche Seiler, Margaret Anderson, Mildred Uhling, Agnes Senda, Monica White, coach Allen King, Mildred Pfau, Dorothy Bahme, Rose Zenn, and chaperone Rachel Becker. (Courtesy of the Struthers Bicentennial Committee.)

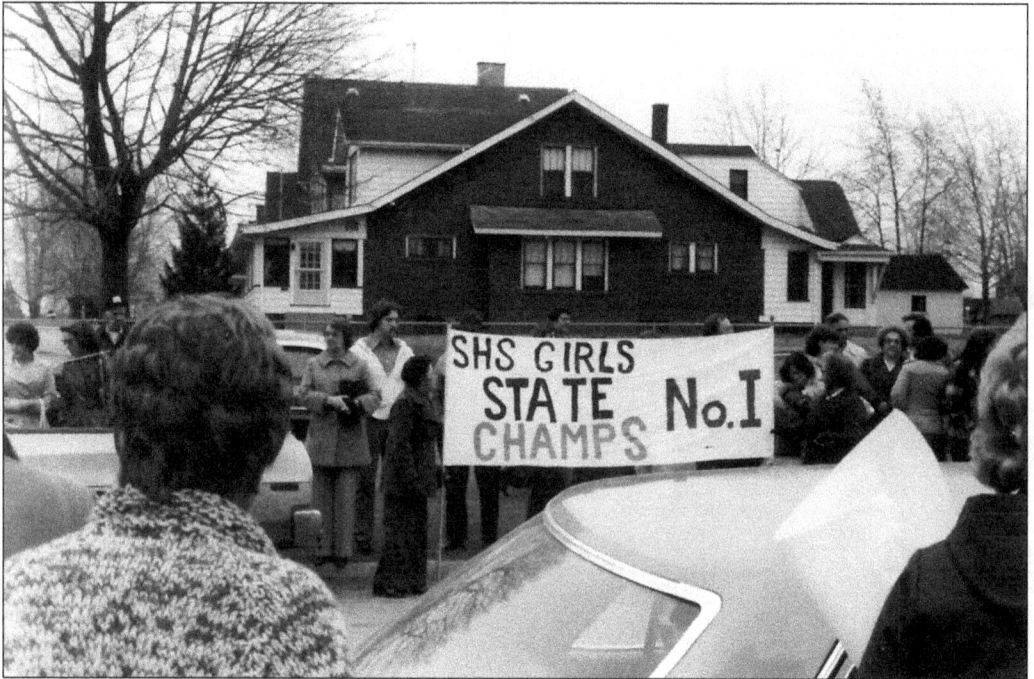

The 1978 Struthers High School girls' basketball team, coached by Dick Prest, won the class AAA state championship. Fans noisily greeted the Lady Wildcats return with as close to a ticker tape parade as Struthers can get, showing that these times were fun for the team, the school, and the community. Members of the team pose with their state trophy in the high school field house. Bonnie Beachy (fourth from left) was named the tournament's most valuable player. Beachy also reached the 1,000-point mark for her career that season.

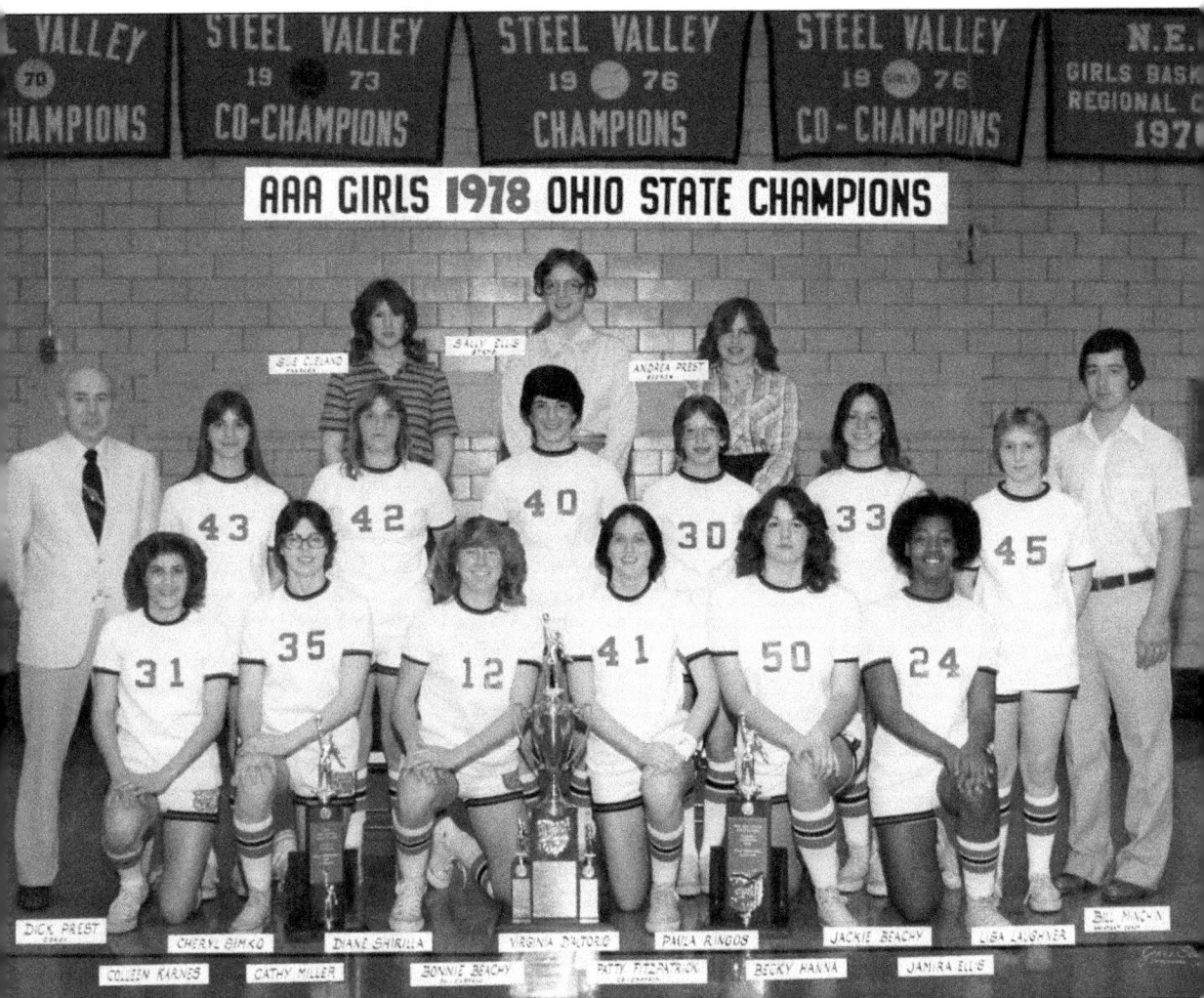

Championship teams inspire greatness for team members and those who watch. This team started the season as defending Steel Valley Conference champions and had a regular season record of 17 wins and one loss. Pictured from left to right are (first row) Colleen Karnes, Cathy Miller, cocaptain Bonnie Beachy, cocaptain Patty Fitzpatrick, Becky Hanna, and Jamira Ellis; (second row) coach Dick Prest, Cheryl Simko, Diane Shirilla, Virginia D'Altorio, Paula Ringos, Jackie Beachy, Lisa Laughner, and assistant coach Bill Minchin; (third row) manager Sue Cleland, statistician Sally Ellis, and scorer Andrea Prest. (Courtesy of Struthers High School.)

In the 1920s, the Struthers Athletic Club semiprofessional football team played on Shaffer Field where Yallech Lumber Company later stood. The 1924 squad includes (first row) Buck Irwin, P. Newman, Frank Stonequest, Fred Pichitino, James Daley, J. Lawlor, Joe Pogen, S. Hungerford, Phil Brown, Calte McMullen, J. Baker, John White, and Bill Harvey; (second row) John Shaffer, Tex Lawlor, Red Donlin, Lacky McClaren, and manager Sim Earich. (Courtesy of the Struthers Athletic Club.)

This is the 1937 Struthers High School football squad, whose record was 3-4-1. Players include (first row) Pep Babich, Patsy Pasquelle, Chester Delsignore, Pete Gordon, and Butch Bero; (second row) Emil "Windy" Elias, Pete Kuba, Vince Marosovich, and Vince Markesevich; (third row) Joe Marosovich, Mike "Flash" Mestrovich, Steve Elash, Frank Benson, John Mihalko, Jim Thompson, Tex Boyarko, Chuck Kimmel, Bert Tombo, Pete Suhey, and Joseph Macejko.

96

In 1936, members of the Struthers High School marching band were fitted for their first band uniforms. Pictured here are band leader Mr. Pletincks, superintendent of schools Mr. Zuber, principal Mr. Gabriel, first drum major Mike Opsitnick, and second drum major Albert Kopp. Band members are (first row) Arlene Wolfgang, LaVerne Guthrie, Maxine Turnbull, Harold Yauman, James LaPaze, and LaVelle Sprague; (second row) Bill Norling, Bill Jones, Robert Black, and Lois Mallery; (third row) Paul Havahou, Franklin Thompson, and Joe Horne; (fourth row) Jack McCelland, Glwyn Lewis, Bill Mackin, Sam Rossano, and Ruth Kimmell. Below, the 1972 marching band is poised and ready to take the field, also in newly purchased uniforms. The Struthers High School Band Booster Club spearheaded the fund-raising for the band shell dedicated in 1970. (Courtesy of Gene's Studio.)

There are many great athletes in the Struthers High School Hall of Fame. John Gerak, a 1988 Struthers High School graduate, played fullback and guard at Pennsylvania State University. As cocaptain his senior year there, Gerak said, "Hard work always paid off . . . And now when I work out, I'm just thinking about my hometown." After graduation, he was drafted 57th by the Minnesota Vikings and later played for the St. Louis Rams. He now practices law in Cleveland where he lives with his family. (Courtesy of John Gerak.)

Stephen Belichick (1919–2005), Struthers High School class of 1936, played football for Western Reserve University and the Detroit Lions. He coached at Hiram College, Vanderbilt University, the University of North Carolina, and the United States Naval Academy. In 2006, his book *Football Scouting Methods* was the second-most sought after out-of-print book. His son Bill is the only head coach in National Football League history to win three Super Bowls in four years, between 2001 and 2004. (Courtesy of Struthers High School.)

Bob Cene Park

Struthers residents enjoy baseball. In town, the Bob Cene Sports Complex has three major-league proportion lighted baseball diamonds. Built on the former Struthers Coke Works site, it is a great spot to enjoy a game today. Credit for the reclamation of this brown field goes to the late Bob Cene Sr., his sons Bob Jr. and Paul, and Jim DiBacco. (Courtesy of Youngstown Class B Baseball.)

This early Struthers Athletic Club team's players, from left to right, are (first row) Lesogonich and Paulansky; (second row) Speich, Jones, Orenic, Bochenek, and Gentile; (third row) Planey, Venglarcik, Markovich, Lesogonich, Paulansky, and Evans; (fourth row) George Roskos, Passek, Pogacnik, Zaluski, Elash, Braydich, and Novotony.

An even earlier team from 1909 was coed and posed in front of the Hanley House. Players are (first row) Mike Pidick, Earl Brace, Bill Mackin, and Bill Mohr; (second row) John Hanley, Jim Slaven, and Tom Richards; (third row) Tillie Hirt, Mary Slaven, Ralph Metts, Frances Mackin, Kate Hanley, Emma Mohr, and Kate Mohr.

Andy Kosco, a 1959 Struthers High School graduate and sports hall of fame member, was signed by the Detroit Tigers as an amateur free agent in 1959. In his Major League Baseball career, he also played with the Minnesota Twins, New York Yankees, Los Angeles Dodgers, Milwaukee Brewers, California Angels, Boston Red Sox, and Cincinnati Reds, retiring in 1974. (Courtesy of Andy Kosco.)

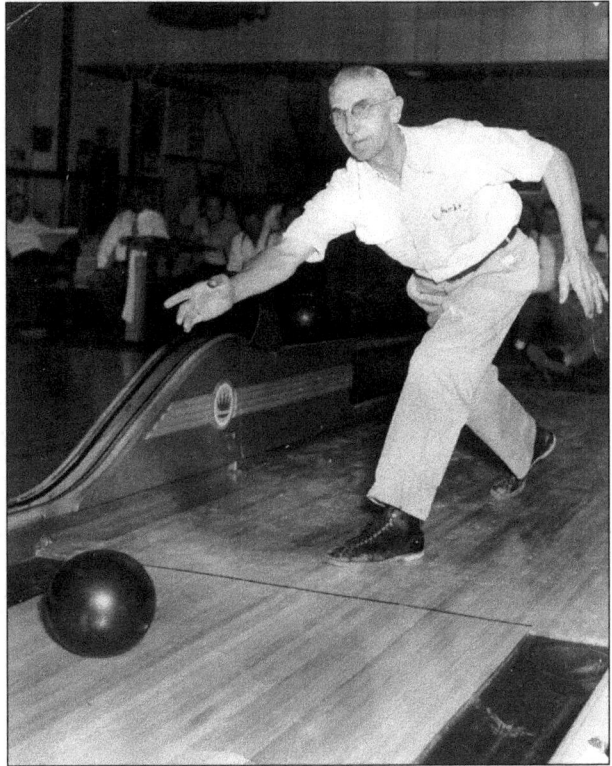

History can trace bowling back to ancient Egypt, Finland, Yemen, and much later, Germany. It is a favorite pastime for many residents, and leagues are full at all the alleys each fall and winter. At right is bowler Jack Almer at the Bowladrome Lanes on State Street. He once bowled two 300 games in one set. Below, these lady bowlers pause for the photographer while traveling to play in Columbus. Team members are Mabel Orlando, Mabel Tilly, Mary Minghetti, Julia Minghetti, and Mildred Raybuck. (Courtesy of the Struthers Athletic Club.)

Another celebration parades along Bridge Street in downtown Struthers. Through the years, the Fourth of July is a popular time to remember the good things about living in America. In 1989, these twirlers (below) help the city to do that, as they march along Poland Avenue.

At Lake Hamilton stands the Peace Keepers Memorial in memory of the 14 Ohio servicemen killed in the October 23, 1983, attack on the U.S. Marine Headquarters in Beirut, Lebanon. Marine corporal Edward Johnston, Struthers High School class of 1978, was killed in that attack. "Some people spend an entire lifetime wondering if they made a difference. The Marines don't have that problem," said Pres. Ronald Reagan in 1985.

In 2006, the Struthers Veterans Memorial was rededicated. The original veterans' memorial was a little-acknowledged but not forgotten hunk of limestone from Bessemer, placed in 1951 in front of the Struthers High School field house to honor World War II veterans. Starting about 2004, a group of less than 20 men and women worked more than two years to embellish this site that few had really noticed in the last 50 years.

The memorial now has a backdrop of waving flags, including the United States of America's, the State of Ohio's, and the POW/MIA's. Flanking it were six columns commemorating each service branch and all veterans. Committee chairman Gene Yuhasz (left) and member Paul Ringos seem pleased with the results at the dedication ceremony.

During the ceremony, speakers were introduced by Laddie Fedor. In this photograph, benefactor Tony Lariccia salutes the veterans. Speeches were also given by Mayor Daniel Mamula, state representative John Boccieri, Mahoning County commissioner Anthony Traficanti, and superintendent of Struthers schools Sandra DiBacco. In the crowd were veterans of wars, conflicts, operations, peace, and those who loved them. Afterwards, the generations streamed onto the lawn and around the memorial to mingle and remember.

What are holidays without a special night out at a favorite restaurant? In this 1991 photograph, Santa Claus visits with the staff and patrons of Marchionda's Restaurant on Fifth Street.

Mavar's chef and carver, C. D. Hurst, is at the buffet.

Religious traditions are also celebrated. In this 1909 photograph, the children of Holy Trinity Catholic Church who received the sacrament of First Holy Communion, one of the sacraments of initiation in the church, pose with Fr. Emil Sloupsky.

The Independent Order of Odd Fellows, Struthers Lodge No. 933, was founded in 1915 with 27 members and grew to 90 by the end of the year. Charter members are pictured here. Guided by friendship, love, and truth, this organization aims to serve less fortunate persons. They purchased their lodge at 99 Poland Avenue in 1920. This hall has significant historical connections. It was originally built as a home for Thomas Struthers then owned by John Struthers and later by Dr. William Morrison.

The Odd Fellows is a worldwide organization that, "Visits the sick, buries the dead, relieves the distressed and educates the orphan." Known for their breakfasts and dinners, this later photograph shows the Odd Fellows and their women's affiliate, the Rebekah Lodge. Everett McCreary, a longtime member, was honored in 1992. He held many offices in the lodge, including noble grand.

Struthers Historical Society was chartered by Secretary of State Ted W. Brown in 1978. Marian Kutlesa was the first president. Its work over the years has been for preservation and celebration. Here the front sign is decorated for a rotary open house at Christmastime. The beautiful gardens celebrating spring and summer are maintained by member Laddie Fedor. (Courtesy of Marian Kutlesa.)

Six

THIS AND THAT

There is so much history that not only does it not fit into this book but there are also many interesting points that do not fit neatly into the previous chapters. This final chapter gives a potpourri of Struthers trivia. "Through the halls of Struthers High School / Loud our praises ring / For to this, our Alma Mater / Always we will sing. / Here's to Struthers, / Hail to thee. / Now we pledge our loyalty. / And we trust we'll ne'er forget you, / True to you we'll be," are the words to the Struthers High School alma mater song. The song was composed by Dorothy Wigfall Green, Struthers High School class of 1945, before her graduation. The wildcat pictured here is the school mascot breaking through the wall of the high school field house. It is an inspiring site.

Struthers High School Memorial Gymnasium
Struthers, Ohio

The Struthers High School Memorial Gymnasium was built in memory of those who died in World War II. This thoroughly modern gymnasium hosted its first basketball game on December 18, 1951, between Struthers and Woodrow Wilson. Built with 1,008 backed seats and 2,000 bench seats, it is a splendid venue for physical education classes, sporting events, rallies, concerts, fairs, exhibitions, and even the Aut Mori Grotto Circus.

COMPLIMENTS OF

WKTL
90.7 FM

STRUTHERS, OHIO

ROBERT MALANCHUS
FACULTY DIRECTOR

"Keys to learning" inspired the call letters for WKTL-90.7 FM. Owned and operated by Struthers High School, the radio station went on the air on September 13, 1965. It was the first high school all-student radio station in the country. Speech teacher Stephen Gercevich was instrumental in starting this unique laboratory for students. This photograph is of the original WKTL radio tower.

September 15, 1990, was recognized by the Ohio State Senate as Struthers Day. In their proclamation, Senators Stanley Aronoff and Harry Meshel recognized, "The optimism and spirit of cooperation found among the residents of Struthers have not only helped the city gain a well-deserved reputation as a friendly, pleasant, and productive place in which to live and work, but have also ensured the continued success and prosperity of this fine community."

Pictured here are the Snappy Snippers Garden Club. From left to right are Dolly Jackson, Penny Zremsky, unidentified, unidentified, Rose Horney, unidentified, Rita Gough, and Marlene Donnelly. Another garden club, one of the first in Struthers, was the Yellow Creek Garden Club, founded in 1933 with a mission to stimulate the knowledge and love of gardening, to aid in the protection of native trees, shrubs, and flowers, and to encourage civic planning.

Speed Up Your Fun With
ISALY KLONDIKES

Rich, smooth Vanilla Ice Cream heavily coated all over
with quality chocolate. Better than ever before. With
each Pink Center Klondike, you receive another one
FREE.

Meet Your Friends Here for Lunch

Enjoy the friendly, courteous service and tempting foods
at your Isaly Stores. Keeping you happy is always a
pleasure.

Isaly's

ENDS THE QUEST FOR THE BEST

"I scream, you scream, we all scream for ice cream"
could be Isaly's motto. This 1928 advertisement
helps recall the Klondike's and "skyscraper"
ice-cream cones among the other dairy products
from Isaly's. Locations were throughout the valley
and the "Big Isaly's" was on Mahoning Avenue in
Youngstown. Here is the downtown Struthers store
being dug out of the blizzard of 1950. Later there was
a store at the Fifth Street Plaza.

On November 25, 1950, 20.7 inches of snow fell. This storm brought snow to the entire Buckeye state and is still the largest snowfall recorded in Struthers in 24 hours. Sitting in the huge snowbanks are Rose Banozic (right) and Louise "Weezie" Frank. Banozic tells the story of how on this snow-filled day after Thanksgiving, the busses were not running. They had no telephone to call ahead, so she and her sister Minnie walked to work at the Dollar Bank only to discover it was closed. Never in their wildest imaginations did they think it would be closed. "We were so happy! It wasn't even hard to walk back home. It didn't bother us at all." (Courtesy of Rose Ringos.)

With the Big Ten championship and a trip to the Rose Bowl on the line, the weekend following this 1950 storm the Ohio State University–University of Michigan "snow bowl" game was played in Columbus. During the game, temperatures hovered at five degrees, winds whipped at 40 miles per hour, and there were 27 total yards gained and not one first down. The University of Michigan won 9-3. Seen here is a bird's-eye view of the horseshoe that day. (Courtesy of the Ohio State University.)

Meine's Flower Shop is pictured here after a school bus failed to negotiate the stop and turn at the bottom of Bridge Street, crashing and damaging the store's front window and wall. The 1980 accident was attributed to icy road conditions.

There are no cemeteries in Struthers. According to the television show *Jeopardy*, Struthers is the only town in the United States that does not have a cemetery. Although there is a legend that a servant girl is buried in an unmarked grave in Yellow Creek Park, Struthers has no independent or church-owned cemetery. This gravestone is the marker at Poland Cemetery for the John Struthers family.

In this undated photograph, the man on the far right is William Duff Struthers and the one on the far left is Earl Struthers. The gentlemen are descendents of John Struthers after whom the town got its name.

On Easter Sunday, March 23, 1913, a light rain began to fall, turning torrential for the next 48 hours and not stopping until Thursday morning. The storm was even worse in other parts of the state, but Struthers suffered widespread damage. Although some area homes suffered losses, the industries along the river incurred extensive damage. There the waters stood several feet deep on the mill floors, covering machinery and furnaces. The railroads and street railway system both stopped. Stanni Persham, a boy from Struthers, was killed when the bank of the Yellow Creek collapsed where he was standing. During the flood of 1913, the Mahoning River crested at 22 feet. The top picture shows the downtown area looking toward the impassable bridge down the street.

In 1938, the post office moved to this impressive new building on top of Bridge Street hill. In 1878, the town's first postal service was located in Alfred G. S. Parker's drugstore. It then moved at least two more times before this permanent home was built. Interestingly, home deliveries were initiated in 1921 and until the mid-1950s two home deliveries were made daily.

This picture is of the St. Anthony DiPadova Auxiliary, founded in 1928 to honor their patron saint. Through the years, they have sponsored sport leagues, contributed to charitable causes, and offered prayerful support. From left to right are (first row) Edith Pasquale, Julia Visingardi, Eleanor Stoich, Judge Robert Kalafut, Arlene DeChellis, and Rosie Hollen; (second row) Claudia DeGennaro, Theresa Colista, Joanne Kalbasky, Theresa Modarelli, Judge James Lanzo, Carmel Quattro, and Rose DiBacco.

In 1980, councilmen Joseph Vlosich and Walter Zaluski contacted Sally Struthers to determine if she was related to the city's founding fathers. Although her letter did not illuminate any genealogical connection, local historians reportedly felt that there is more than a chance she could be related to John Struthers. She wrote, "For the city of Struthers I put on my tuxedo to lend importance to this astute statement: 'It takes one to know one.'"

The Ku Klux Klan, which, according to the *Youngstown Vindicator*, espoused white supremacy, nativism, and anti-Catholicism, appeared in the Midwest in the early 1920s about the time this picture was taken. Residents recall burned crosses at Helena Street and at the Holy Trinity Church pavilion. Although supposedly apolitical, its candidates won mayoral elections in Youngstown, Niles, Warren, Girard, and Struthers in 1923. They were unsuccessful in gaining control of the United Presbyterian Church.

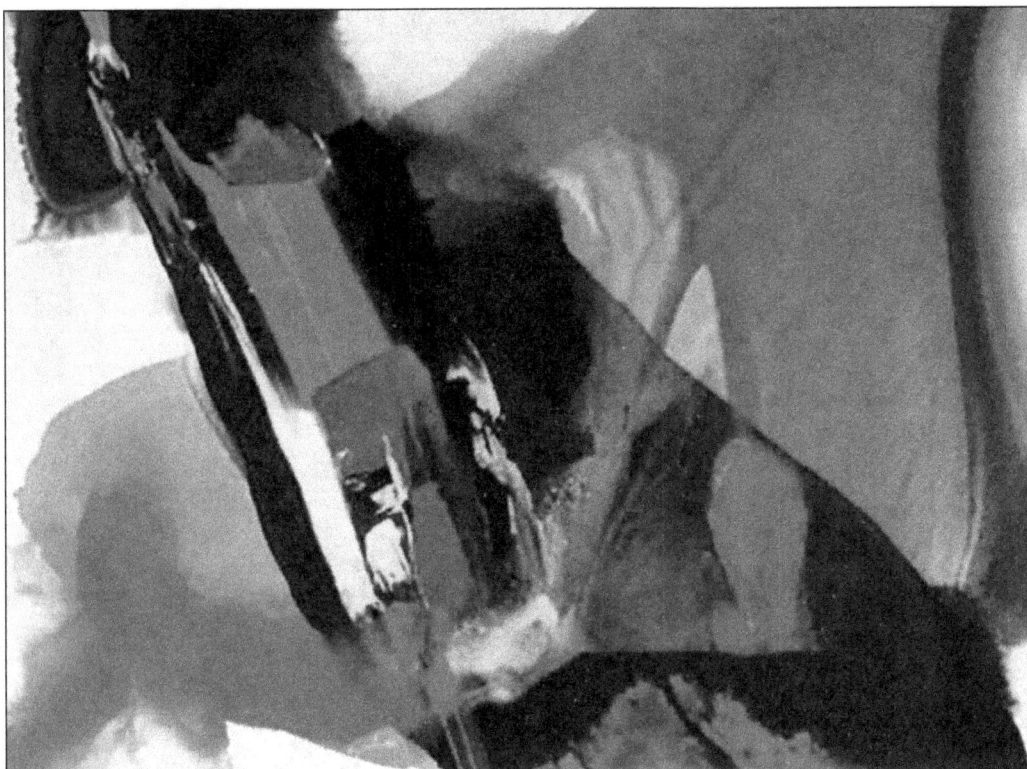

Paul Jenkins, who was born in 1923 in Kansas City, Missouri, and is a Struthers High School graduate, is world renowned for his abstract expressionism and flowing paint technique. His large powerfully colorful canvases represent American abstraction after World War II. He is also known for the process of controlled paint pouring and canvas manipulation. The Butler Institute of American Art owns several of his paintings. Pictured here is *Phenomena Prime Meridian* (2003).

Nadyne Herrick, longtime owner, publisher, and editor of the *Struthers, Campbell and Lowellville Journal* was Jenkin's mother. She and her husband bought the paper after moving from Kansas City. First located beneath the Penner's Furniture building, the company later moved to the Yallech Lumber building located at the entrance to Yellow Creek Park. Here mother and son are pictured together.

This is the Struthers Athletic Club, or Struthers A. C., a familiar landmark that was located in downtown Struthers. It preserved irreplaceable memorabilia from Struthers High School athletics and other Struthers teams. For use in this book, John Gingery shared memorabilia that he was able to save following the fire. (Courtesy of the Struthers Athletic Club.)

In 2005, fire destroyed the Struthers Athletic Club along with the Wagon Wheel and Sulmona Valley Club. Beyond keeping memorabilia, the club was a place for food, drink, and celebrations over the decades. The top picture shows members and guests enjoying an evening of fun and dancing. The 1940 photograph below shows members at an outdoor gathering. (Courtesy of the Struthers Athletic Club.)

The Thomas Struthers Memorial Library was dedicated by board of trustees chairman Ben Defendeifer as a branch of the Public Library of Youngstown and Mahoning County. It was presented debt free to the community in September 1957. The facilities and holdings were equaled in only a few communities of comparable size. Before this building was completed, the library operated out of the Knights of Pythias building on South Bridge Street for 20 years.

These are members of the Slovak parish, Holy Trinity Catholic Church, in their native costumes. Eighty percent of Slovak Americans were Roman Catholic, whose churches and parochial schools were important to them in part because of a long history of religious suppression in Europe. Once a neighborhood harbored enough families, a parish committee was organized, and the bishop petitioned to establish a Slovak nationality church.

The gentleman chef pictured on Nabisco Cream of Wheat is Henry Galbreath. Reportedly, Galbreath was paid $5 for the photograph of his handsome smile that later appeared on every box of Nabisco Cream of Wheat. Born in Detroit in 1850, he was the son of a freed slave whose name was that of the family that owned his father in the South. He studied early in his life to be a chef and was a champion cook on the New York Central Railroad lines. During that time, he met Emery Mapes, who was struggling to introduce his breakfast porridge to the American public, and Mapes asked to take his picture. Later Galbreath owned and operated a coal company in Struthers.

Alma Frankforter was the seamstress who lived at 50 Terrace Street for 93 years. Her home houses the Struthers Historical Society. This textile collection, housed at the Struthers Historical Society, is representative of period clothing. Other valuable and informative collections are from personal and professional donations that document much of Struthers's history, including the Hopewell Furnace, the Youngstown Sheet and Tube Company, the *Spirit of Struthers* World War II bomber, Struthers High School yearbooks, and the *Struthers Journal*. (Courtesy of Marian Kutlesa.)

The Elmton is credited with being the first pizza place in Struthers and is still operating in 2008. It also offers a full menu. Located at Elm and Fifth Streets, it was established in 1945 by John Walters. Pictured here from left to right are (behind the bar) John A. Walters and Lucille Birmingham; (seated) Harry Fennern, Carl Lanksbury, John Mills, Frank Androsik, and Clarence "Pappy" Andre. (Courtesy of Elmton.)

BIBLIOGRAPHY

Beelen, George, and Martha Pallante, eds. *An Ethnic Encyclopedia: The Peopling of the Mahoning Valley*. Ohio Cultural Alliance, 1996.

Bruno, Robert. *Steelworker Alley: How Class Works in Youngstown*. Ithaca, NY: ILR Press, an imprint of Cornell University Press, 1999.

Butler, Joseph. *History of Youngstown and the Mahoning Valley Ohio*. Chicago: American Historical Society, 1921.

Emerson, Ken. *Doo-dah! Stephen Foster and the Rise of American Popular Culture*. New York: Simon and Schuster, 1997.

"An Industrial Water Supply for the Youngstown District." *Iron Trade Review*, December 1908.

Kutlesa, Marian. "A History of Home." Unpublished manuscript, 1986.

Mallery, Harry. "Bridge Street 1899." Unpublished manuscript, Struthers Historical Society archives, 1971.

Royster, Jacqueline Jones. *Profiles of Ohio Women: 1803–2003*. Athens, OH: Ohio University Press, 2003.

Sanderson, Thomas. *Twentieth Century History of Mahoning County and Representative Citizens*. Chicago: 1902.

Struthers Bicentennial Committee. *Struthers, Ohio Cradle of Steel*. Struthers Bicentennial Committee, 1976.

Struthers High School Alumni Directory. Holiday, FL: Alumni Research, 1998.

Struthers Total Environmental Education Program. *Struthers: Prologue–Epilogue*. Struthers, OH: Struthers Total Environmental Education Program, 1975.

Struthers Veterans and Civic Association. *The Cradle of Steel, Struthers, Ohio 1804–1948*. Struthers Veterans and Civic Association, 1948.

Youngstown Sheet and Tube Company. *Fifty Years in Steel: The Youngstown Sheet and Tube Company*. Youngstown, OH: Youngstown Sheet and Tube Company, 1950.

Youngstown Vindicator. *These Hundred Years: A Chronicle of the Twentieth Century*. Youngstown Vindicator, 2000.

Visit us at
arcadiapublishing.com